THE CLASH
MUSIC THAT MATTERS

BY TONY FLETCHER

D0525211

OMNIBUS PRESS

LONDON / NEW YORK / PARIS / SYDNEY / COPENHAGEN / BERLIN / MADRID / TOKYO

1952
AUGUST 21

John Mellor, the future Joe Strummer, born in Ankara, Turkey. The son of a diplomat, he attends boarding school in England.

1975

Jones, who has been playing guitar for three years in such glam-influenced bands as Schoolgirl, the Delinquents and Little Queenie, forms a new group deliberately intended to upset the status quo: London SS, with Tony James.

1974

Mellor renames himself Joe Strummer ("because I can only play all six string at once, or none at all"), and returns to London from Newport Art School in Wales. Out of a squat in Maida Vale, he forms the 101'ers, who quickly make a name on London's thriving "pub rock" circuit.

1955
MAY 30

Nicky Headon born in Bromley, Kent.

1955
JUNE 26

Mick Jones born in Clapham, South London.

1970
SUMMER

Mellor moves to London to attend Central School of Art. He breaks from his past by taking the name Woody (as in, Guthrie) and taking up busking.

1955
DECEMBER 15

Paul Simonon born in Brixton, South London.

1975
AUGUST

Jones and James meet Bernie Rhodes at the Nashville in Kensington. Rhodes, who has been involved in setting up the Sex Pistols, offers to manage them.

1976
APRIL

The Sex Pistols open for the 101'ers at the Nashville Rooms. Strummer immediately sees his current band as "yesterday's papers." By coincidence, Jones, Simonon and second guitarist Keith Leven are in the audience. Fans of the Pistols, they also look up to Strummer as a possible vocalist for their own band.

1976
JANUARY

Simonon, a visual artist, accompanies an aspiring drummer friend to one of London SS's many auditions. He tries out as singer but having no musical talent, is rejected.

1976
JUNE

Strummer joins what will soon become the Clash. Rhodes takes a lease on a former gin factory in Camden Town; as Rehearsal Rehearsals, it becomes the group's base.

1976
SPRING

Tony James and new drummer Rat Scabies leave London SS to form the Damned. Jones recruits Simonon after running into him on the Portobello Road, encouraging him to learn an instrument; he eventually takes up the bass.

1976
JULY 4

With Keith Levene as second guitarist and Terry Chimes on drums, The Clash play their debut gig, opening for the Sex Pistols in Sheffield.

1976
AUGUST 31

Strummer, Simonon and Rhodes are present when West London's annual Notting Hill Carnival ends in a pitched battle between West Indian youth and the police. The event becomes the inspiration for the first Clash single 'White Riot.'

1976
SEPTEMBER 20

The Clash play as part of the London Punk Festival at the 100 Club, alongside the Sex Pistols, Subway Sect and Siouxsie and the Banshees. Levene having departed, it is their first gig as a four-piece.

1977
MARCH

The Clash release their first single 'White Riot'/'1977.' It quickly becomes a punk anthem, though it only grazes the top 40.

1976
DECEMBER

In disagreements over the group's overt political stance, Terry Chimes quits on the eve of the 'Anarchy In The UK Tour,' which sees the Clash bottom of the bill to the Sex Pistols, the Damned and Johnny Thunders' Heartbreakers. Rob Harper takes Chimes' place, but most shows are canceled as a result of anti-Pistols/punk rock hysteria.

1977
JANUARY 27

The Clash sign a five-album, £100,000 deal with CBS Records. The decision to go with a major label is criticized by many as contrary to punk rock's ethics.

1976
NOVEMBER

The Clash record a demo tape for Polydor, "produced" by Guy Stevens, who spends most of the time at the pub.

The Clash are the subject of a major profile in *Melody Maker* by Caroline Coon.

1977
JANUARY-FEBRUARY

With live sound engineer Mickey Foote as producer and Terry Chimes – credited as Tory Crimes – agreeing to record the songs as a favour to the group, The Clash record their first album in fifteen days.

1977
JANUARY 1

The Clash appear on the cover of *Sounds* as the music paper's "pick for '77."

1977
SEPTEMBER

Despite the lyrics, CBS releases 'Complete Control,' production credited to Jamaican reggae icon Lee 'Scratch' Perry. Headon's first recording with the band, it is considered by many to the Clash's best early recording; the single spends one week inside the Top 30.

1977
MAY

The "White Riot" tour of the UK sees Nicky Headon joining as new and permanent drummer. He is nicknamed "Topper" for his resemblance to the monkey on the cover of the British weekly comic of the same name. Support band the Jam quit after violence flares at the London Rainbow; the Buzzcocks and Slits continue on with the tour.

CBS releases 'Remote Control' from *The Clash* against the group's wishes. It doesn't chart. Strummer and Jones write 'Complete Control,' a none-too-thinly-veiled attack on the record label, in response.

1977
APRIL

The Clash is released, reaching number 12 in the British charts. With thirteen Strummer-Jones compositions and a ground-breaking punk-reggae version of Junior Murvin's 'Police & Thieves' it is considered by many, despite or because of its basic sound, to be the definitive punk statement.

The *New Musical Express* gives away a free Clash EP featuring an unreleased song 'Capital Radio' along with an interview with the band.

1977
OCTOBER/NOVEMBER/DECEMBER

The 'Out Of Control' Tour travels the length and breadth of the UK. In Glasgow, Strummer and Simonon are arrested and jailed overnight after a confrontation with security.

1978
APRIL

The Clash appear at the first Carnival Against the Nazis, promoted by Rock Against Racism and the Anti-Nazi League, in Victoria Park, Hackney. The crowd is in the tens of thousands. The group is in the midst of being filmed for a movie, *Rude Boy*, which will eventually be released in 1980; actor Ray Gange, playing an archetypal dissatisfied British youth/Clash fan, is shot at the Carnival in several scenes of 'cinema verite.'

1978
FEBRUARY

A new single, 'Clash City Rockers,' is sped up at the mastering stage. Producer Mickey Foote is fired as a result. The single fails to make the top 30.

Joe Strummer and Mick Jones travel to Kingston, Jamaica. They come back with the song 'Safe European Home,' which will open the Clash's second LP.

1978
MAY

The Clash start recording their second album in London with American producer Sandy Pearlman. The process eventually ends in San Francisco and New York, leading to criticisms that the band is selling out to the American rock market.

1978
MARCH

Headon, Simonon and three others are arrested for firing air-rifles on the roof of their Camden Town Rehearsal Rehearsals studio. Strummer and Jones later write 'Guns On The Roof' about the incident.

1978
JUNE-JULY

The 'Out On Parole' tour travels through the UK.

1978
NOVEMBER

Give 'Em Enough Rope, The Clash's second LP, is finally released, to mixed reviews. It nonetheless makes number two on the UK charts while the single 'Tommy Gun' is their first to make the top 20.

1979
FEBRUARY

A brief tour of the States in support of *Give 'Em Enough Rope*, the band's first official American release.

'English Civil War,' the second single from *Give 'Em Enough Rope*, released. The B-side features a powerful cover of the reggae song 'Pressure Drop.'

1979
JULY

A re-packaged edition of debut LP *The Clash*, including many of the subsequent non-LP single tracks, is released in America, with 'I Fought The Law' selected as the band's first Stateside single.

1979
JULY-SEPTEMBER

London Calling is recorded at Wessex Studios in London. Despite his transgression at the band's first ever recording, Guy Stevens is hired as producer. The Clash ultimately record 19 songs across many genres – and insist that every one of them makes the final cut.

1979
MAY

To coincide with the election of new Prime Minister Margaret Thatcher, 'The Cost of Living' EP is released, co-produced by the Clash and Bill Price. Lead track is a cover of the Bobby Fuller Four's 'I Fought The Law.'

1978
NOVEMBER/DECEMBER

The 'Sort It Out' tour has the Clash playing continental Europe and the UK through the end of the year.

Manager Bernie Rhodes is fired; he takes legal action that sees the band expelled from its Camden rehearsal room. Simonon's girlfriend, the journalist Caroline Coon, initially replaces Rhodes, but the group soon hires Peter Jenner and Andrew King of Blackhill, Pink Floyd's original managers.

1979
MAY-JUNE

Moving into Vanilla Studios in Pimlico, the Clash undertake daily rehearsals, formulating the songs that will become *London Calling*.

1980
APRIL

'Train In Vain (Stand By Me)', the "hidden" disco-funk track sung by Mick Jones at the end of *London Calling*, becomes The Clash's first American hit single.

1980
JANUARY

London Calling is released in the United States. It makes the Top 30 there in March.

1979
DECEMBER

The single and double album *London Calling* are released within a week of each other in the UK, to enormous acclaim.

1980
MAY-JUNE

The 'Sixteen Tons' tour resumes through Europe and the UK.

1979
SEPTEMBER-OCTOBER

The 'Take The Fifth' Tour of North America, 23 dates with opening acts including the Undertones, Bo Diddley, and Sam and Dave.

1980
JANUARY-MARCH,

The 'Sixteen Tons' tour of the UK and USA sees reggae MC Mikey Dread frequently join the band onstage. On a day off in Manchester, the Clash with Dread record the reggae song 'Bankrobber' as what they hope will be the first in a series of monthly single releases. CBS refuses to go along with the concept.

1980
OCTOBER

The Black Market Clash compilation, comprising mostly are B-sides and dub versions, is released in the USA only.

1981
JANUARY

Sandanista! is released in the USA, where it will eventually peak at number 24 in the chart, three places higher than *London Calling*.

'Hitsville UK' is released as a single, but fails in the UK even to make the top 50.

Blackhill Management is fired and Bernie Rhodes rehired as manager.

1980
AUGUST

After its appearance on a Dutch B-Side meets with great enthusiasm, CBS relents and releases Bankrobber' as a UK single. It makes number 12 in the UK charts but the band keeps to an early promise not to appear on *Top of The Pops*; the show uses its female dancers to 'interpret' the track instead.

1981
MAY-JUNE

Eight scheduled shows at Bond's International Casino in New York City turn into 17 when the fire department cites the opening night for over-crowding. The venue's Times Square location and the group's growing popularity in America turns the extended run into a media frenzy and helps cement the Clash's status in the States.

1981
APRIL-MAY

The 'Impossible Mission' tour travels through Europe.

Sandanista!'s opening song, 'The Magnificent Seven' is released as a single. An instrumental 12" remix 'The Magnificent Dance' captures the sound of the emerging hip-hop scene and is embraced by black radio in New York.

1980
DECEMBER

Sandanista! is released in the UK. Recorded in five studios in three countries, and named for the Nicaraguan revolutionary movement, the triple album, at single LP price, takes the *London Calling* concept to a possibly illogical conclusion, and is met with mostly negative reviews and disappointing sales. 'The Call-Up' precedes its release as a UK Single.

1981
SEPTEMBER

Eight nights at the Theatre Mogador in Paris.

1982
JANUARY-FEBRUARY

First ever tour of the Far East, New Zealand and Australia taxes the group physically. In Australia, Joe Strummer collapses on stage. In Thailand, where the tour ends, Paul Simonon is hospitalized with a fever and the group stays on to look after him. Topper Headon is now addicted to heroin. When Mick Jones presents the band with a 15-song double LP, they reject it.

1982
MAY

Strummer returns from hiding on the eve of *Combat Rock*'s release and insists that Headon is fired for his heroin addiction. Terry Chimes returns as drummer for the imminent American tour.

Combat Rock is released. It peaks at number two in the UK and will spend eight months in the American top 40.

1981
OCTOBER

The 'Radio Clash' tour of the UK concludes with seven nights at the Lyceum in London.

1981
NOVEMBER

'This Is Radio Clash,' a natural musical follow-on from 'The Magnificent Seven', released as a single in various formats and mixes.

1982
APRIL

'Know Your Rights' released as a UK single in advance of *Combat Rock*. It charts poorly in the UK and Bernie Rhodes advises Strummer to go "missing" so he can cancel a poorly-selling Scottish tour. Strummer calls his bluff and goes missing for real, surviving incognito in France for a month.

1982
MARCH-APRIL

Combat Rock is mixed by veteran producer Glyn Johns and reduced to a single, 12-song album.

1982
MAY-JUNE

The 'Casbah Club' tour of America includes five nights at the Hollywood Palladium in Los Angeles.

1982
SEPTEMBER

A double A-side from *Combat Rock* is released. Radio quickly picks up on 'Should I Stay or Should I Go' over 'Straight To Hell' and it becomes the Clash's first UK top 20 hit since 'Bankrobber.' In the USA, the Clash perform both songs on *Saturday Night Live*.

1982
JULY-AUGUST

The 'Casbah Club' tour of the UK restores the group's popularity in their homeland.

1982
OCTOBER

The Clash return to the States as opening band for the Who, a tour that includes several stadiums and helps propel both 'Rock The Casbah' and *Combat Rock* into their respective top 10s.

1982
JUNE

'Rock The Casbah' released as a single. Ironically, it was written and mostly performed by the now-absent Headon. It reaches number 30 in the UK.

1982
AUGUST-SEPTEMBER

The 'Combat Rock' tour of the States features reggae (Burning Spear) and hip-hop (Kurtis Blow) acts for support.

1983
MAY

With Pete Howard on drums, The Clash play four warm-up shows in the States before performing to 150,000 people at the Us Festival in California. Arguments over fees, billing, and profits spill over into a press conference and result in the Clash playing to their biggest audience at their lowest ebb.

1983
JANUARY-FEBRUARY

Strummer produces and directs a silent, black-and-white movie starring Jones and Simonon as opposing gangsters. *Hell W10* eventually sees the light of day in 2003.

1983
AUGUST-SEPTEMBER

Mick Jones is fired during the week of the Notting Hill Carnival. A terse statement is released to the press: "It is felt that Jones had drifted away from the original idea of the Clash." Jones issues a statement denying as much and asserting: "In the future I'll be carrying on in the same way as in the beginning." By the time of the announcement, he has already formed Big Audio Dynamite. The Clash as they have been known and loved are no more.

1983
AUGUST

Rehearsals for a new album grind to a halt in disputes over musical direction. Jones refuses to sign new management contract with Rhodes.

1983
OCTOBER

Strummer and Simonon, with Pete Howard staying on drums, advertise for new members of the Clash. Guitarists Nick Sheppard and Vince White pass the audition.

1985
JUNE-AUGUST

The Clash play sporadic
European festivals. The Greek
Music Festival in Athens on 27
August, in front of 40,000, is their
last. Strummer disappears
immediately afterwards to Spain
for a month.

1984
MARCH

The new Clash plays its first British
show at the Brixton Academy. The
'Out Of Control' tour, as it is called,
will ratchet up some eighty shows
over the course of the year.

1984
JANUARY

The new-look, back-to-
basics Clash plays six
dates in California.

1985
MAY

The Clash undertake a
busking tour of the UK.

1984
DECEMBER

Rhodes and Strummer go to Munich to
record a new Clash album. Pete Howard is
left behind: drums, along with keyboards,
are to be programmed. Rhodes takes a
co-writing credit on the new songs
alongside Strummer.

1985
SEPTEMBER

A single, 'This Is England', is
released alongside the LP *Cut The
Crap*. The single is well-received; the
album is panned. Strummer returns
after the negative reaction to
announce the permanent break-up
of the band called The Clash.

IN

From the punk fury of their 1977 debut *The Clash* to the sprawling global extravaganza of the 1980 triple album *Sandinista!*, The Clash traveled a greater musical distance in a shorter period of time than any rock band since (and maybe even including) The Beatles. Given the unparalleled speed of this musical (r)evolution, and allowing for the band's confrontational (and contradictory) attitudes, it was perhaps no surprise that their most successful album, 1982's *Combat Rock*, also proved to be their swan-song. Another album under a different line-up belatedly followed, but *Cut The Crap* has since been excised from 'official' Clash history as an aberration.

ODUCTION

Five albums then, spanning some sixteen sides of vinyl, in barely five years. Of those albums, *The Clash* is rightly revered as *the* Great British punk statement, while the double album *London Calling* is widely considered an all-time rock'n'roll classic. *Sandinista!*, which caused considerable confusion at the time, grows ever more alluring with age, and *Combat Rock*, though inconsistent, contains the group's biggest hit singles. Even 1978's *Give 'Em Enough Rope*, buried in bad production, has more than its share of moments. Add in a series of groundbreaking singles released in isolation from these albums, a number of noteworthy B-sides, and a penchant for dub versions and extended remixes, and you're looking at one of the most impressive catalogues in modern musical history.

Few would have anticipated this eventual assessment back when The Clash first made headlines, in late 1976 and early 1977, at the vanguard of punk rock. At that point, the London band's simplicity was often mistaken for stupidity. It's true that when The Clash came together, with a genuine desire to kick-start a streetwise musical revolution that would represent and reflect the disaffected British youth of the late Seventies, they played up any working class roots and minimised their musical smarts so as to distance themselves from the rock 'dinosaurs' against whom they were aligned. But behind their self-admitted 'Stalinist' denial of the past (in which 1976 was declared, with a nod to Pol Pot's *very* Stalinist Khmer Rouge, as a musical 'Year Zero') stood some inherently intelligent and creative people.

For Mick Jones, pop music became an obsession in early childhood, manifesting into a teenage love affair with glam and the sobriquet "Rock'n'roll Mick". Subsequent drastic haircuts - and an emphasis on his late teenage home in a tower block above the Westway - failed to mask the South London grammar school boy's skills as a composer, arranger, and guitarist. Fellow South Londoner Paul Simonon was a self-taught bass player and practiced painter whose love of reggae manifested itself throughout the group's career. His solid working class credentials and indisputable good looks marked him as the personification of punk cool. And Joe Strummer, born John Mellor in Turkey as the son of a career diplomat, had demonstrated a passion for traditional rock'n'roll, along with an ability to command an audience, as the dynamic singer for pub rockers The 101ers. After witnessing the audio-visual assault of support group The Sex Pistols in April 1976, Strummer paused to reevaluate his musical direction, and was quickly poached for Jones and Simonon's band by their manager Bernie Rhodes. A former cohort of Malcolm McLaren's, with whom he shared an interest in Situationists and an income from the clothing trade, Rhodes saw himself fulfilling the same Svengali role with The Clash as McLaren purported to with The Sex Pistols. Rhodes proved pivotal to Clash politics and attitude, but as with McLaren, his charges quickly proved themselves perfectly capable of thinking, writing, playing - and finally, conducting business – without him. (Rhodes' return to the fold in 1981 soon led to the demise of The Clash as they were known and loved.)

Jones, Strummer and Simonon found the right drummer only after they had already recorded their first album. Nicky 'Topper' Headon was a Grammar School boy from the southern coastal town of Dover; he had grown up studying jazz and had just come off a stint playing soul for GIs in Germany, but he was equally adept at reggae rim shots, disco hi-hats and the punk rock snare roll. Once Headon joined, The Clash finally felt

complete, and thanks largely to their disparate musical backgrounds, individual ambitions and collective solidarity, the quartet was ready to quickly abandon punk's musically rigidity – though their commitment to the movement's ethos caused continual ethical dilemmas and frequent critical backlashes – and embark upon that unprecedented musical journey. Things started to dissolve internally at precisely the point they came together commercially, but for five years, no other group recorded so often, with such emotional vigor, and such eager disdain for the rules.

Notes:
The Clash album was not released in America until 1979, long after its successor *Give 'Em Enough Rope* had hit the shops, and then with different songs and an altered running order. The group's other albums experienced no such tampering across the various international markets, and when given the long-awaited re-mastering treatment in 1999, were left unadorned by 'bonus' or 'unreleased' tracks - probably because The Clash released just about everything they recorded as they went along. The double album *London Calling* is a single CD; the triple album *Sandinista!* is a double CD; the American 10" EP *Black Market Clash* was eventually expanded into the full-length CD *Super Black Market Clash*. The importance and influence of the group's non-album singles is such that, in the following Guide, they are addressed individually and chronologically; other singles are written about within the albums from which they were taken. All compositions up to and including *London Calling* are by Strummer-Jones unless noted; all compositions on *Sandinista!* and *Combat Rock* are by The Clash unless noted; *Cut The Crap* songs are credited to Strummer-Rhodes.

Album abbreviations as follows:
TCUS – *The Clash* (US)
SBMC – *Super Black Market Clash*
TSOTC – *The Story of The Clash*
TS – *The Singles*
COB – *Clash On Broadway*
TEC – *The Essential Clash*

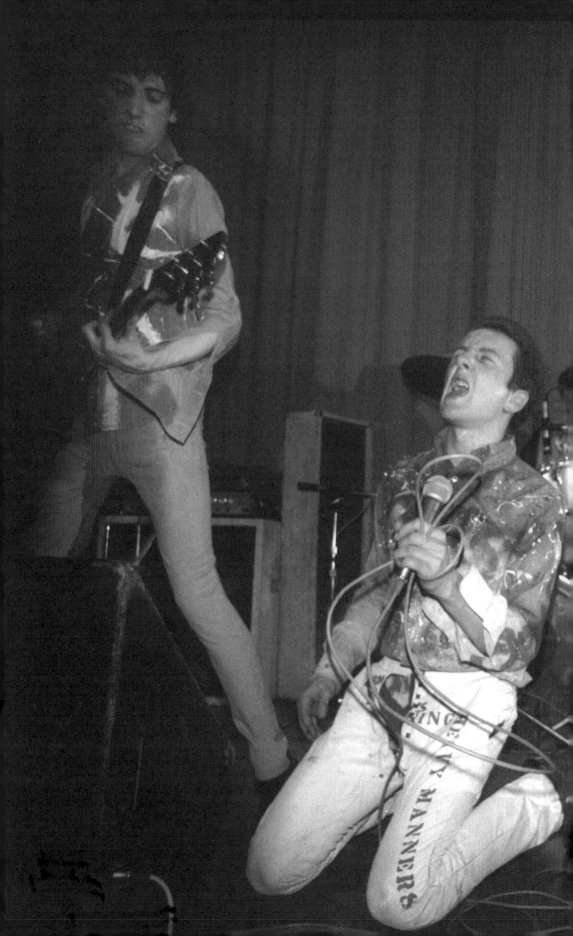

PART I
THE GROUP
RECORDINGS

WHITE RIOT/1977
(UK single March 1977)
The debut single by The Clash was recorded over a three-day weekend beginning January 28, 1977, itself just three days after the group signed a surprise long-term contract with CBS Records. The speed of activity reflected a fear, shared by label and band alike, that other so-called punk groups (notably The Damned, The Stranglers and The Jam) were stealing a march on The Clash; it also reflected the label's desire to unleash their first punk signings before the tabloid furor provoked by The Sex Pistols/Clash 'Anarchy In The UK' (non-)tour of December 1976 died down.

Conversely, the breakneck pace from signing of contract to release of single reflected a relatively casual approach to the 45s market. Absent an American label's need for long-term scheduling, and in an era uncomplicated by promotional videos, rock singles were talked up by the British weekly music papers and then added (or not, as was mostly the case for The Clash) to the BBC's Radio 1 Playlist, after which the process was repeated, and hopefully improved upon, for as long as a band had financial backing.

So, CBS simply dispatched its new signings to the label's Whitfield Street studios in central London, where house engineer Simon Humphrey assisted Micky Foote, live sound engineer for The Clash (and The 101ers before them), in capturing the group's two most overt battle cries in all their raw fury. 'White Riot' had been written about the violent conclusion to the previous August Bank Holiday's Notting Hill Carnival, where Strummer, Simonon and manager Bernie Rhodes had found themselves in the midst of a confrontation between black youth and the police. While the Clash duo eagerly participated in the violence, labeled Britain's biggest 'race riot' since disturbances in the same area back in 1958, they recognised that this was not their struggle. 'White Riot' ably articulated that understanding through

verses that applauded the black man's willingness to "throw a brick" and accused white people of being "too chicken" to act likewise, and a chorus that demanded a "white riot, a riot of my own." Given the politically charged atmosphere in Britain at the time, with the racist National Front making alarming gains at the polls, 'White Riot' was frequently misunderstood – though only by those who failed to comprehend punk in the first place.

'1977' correctly forewarned the coming year as one of potential revolution, or at least of pronounced civil unrest, and in that sense is as important a recording as any in The Clash catalogue. But it was more ambiguous, and thereby open to greater misinterpretation. References to "Knives In West 11" (the group's Notting Hill postcode) and "Sten Guns In Knightsbridge" (the upper class enclave a couple of miles away) appeared to

endorse violence, especially as each phrase appeared on the group's clothing at the time. The chorus "No Elvis, Beatles or the Rolling Stones" appeared equally dogmatic and, as Strummer had feared when he suggested it, would return to haunt the band. He had written it to reflect his acceptance, in leaving The 101ers, that the new groups could not rely on cover versions or past blueprints, but it betrayed a willingness to place shock tactics over lyrical integrity.

In the context of the times, this was understandable. The two songs were set to abrasive, sub two-minute recordings full of piercing, staccato guitars, tin can drums, and shouted choruses; if there were bass speakers in the studio, someone forgot to turn them up. 'White Riot' was ordained with sound effects (a police siren, breaking glass, stomping jackboots and a fire alarm); the opening chords of '1977' betrayed the

chorus line with a riff based closely on The Kinks' 'All Day And All Of The Night'. Insiders seemed disappointed with the single's thin aural quality, barely a step above the group's two previous demo recordings of the same songs, and it was no surprise that it was shunned by radio at the time. But for Joe Public, the single fulfilled its intended incendiary purpose as an invitation to abandon previous perceptions of sonic and musical professionalism, and to join a cultural revolution based instead on energy and emotion. The single's lowly chart position belies just how many people routinely bought 7" singles at the time, and how strongly it influenced those who made the purchase.

WHITE RIOT: Available on TCUS, TS, TSOTC, COB, TEC
1977: Available on SBMC, COB, TEC (U.K. only)

THE CLASH

(UK Album, April 1977)

Recorded and mixed in three sessions of four days apiece in February 1977, *The Clash* is more than just the definitive punk rock statement; it's also one of the most exciting and enduring debut albums in rock'n'roll.

The primary reason for its immediate appeal is relatively obvious: there had never been anything like it before. The previous year, The Ramones' debut album had influenced British punks (including The Clash) with its speaker-shattering, stripped-down simplicity, but much of its sensationalism was wrapped in direct humor, and the New York band made no attempt to anger the political establishment. *The Clash,* on the other hand, from violent sleeve imagery through provocative song titles, presented itself as nothing less than a call to musical and class warfare. Rock fans up and down Great Britain, tired of aloof heroes playing elaborate compositions in vast seated halls – and these fans were often the same young people struggling with the monotony of school, or to find meaningful employment in an increasingly depressed economy– discovered with delight that The Clash spoke *for* them, as opposed *to* them.

Criticism from 'elders' and 'betters' only endorsed the record's appeal. For the thousands captivated by The Clash, the apparent repetition of subject matter served to render the largely unintelligible words

emotionally coherent as a whole; the violent stance reflected in titles like 'Hate And War', 'White Riot' and 'London's Burning' was matched by a contagious emotional energy, the embodiment of punk's purist promise; the lack of musical skill served not as deterrent but inspiration for all who had previously cowed in respect for mid-Seventies guitar gods and their supernatural solos. *The Clash* set children against parents, pupils against teachers, even siblings against siblings. The Clash as a group often spoke of society in terms of "Us Against Them"; *The Clash* as an album delivered on that divide.

The reasons for the album's longevity lie just beneath the surface of its supposed simplicity. Though it was presented partly as a reaction to the overblown prog-rock operas of the mid-Seventies, *The Clash* was very much a concept album. The group members were frequently criticised for over-stating their supposed social disenfranchisement, and it's true that they rewrote their personal histories to avoid any suggestion of prior security or comfort. But it's the very fact that they stepped beyond personal experience to speak, not just for themselves, but in the voice of the *ultimate* urban outcast, that renders the lyrics so eternally effective. Mick Jones said in an interview, shortly before the group signed their record deal, "These songs couldn't be written in any other year," and he was right. Mark P, founder of punk fanzine *Sniffin' Glue*, then wrote of those songs, as they were heard on *The Clash,* that "It's like watching my life in a movie." And he was right, too. *The Clash* will forever tell the story of the desperate, repressed young white male in the faltering, fragmented England of 1977 – and precisely because, in its nihilism, it dares not look further ahead than the present moment, it's never lost its impact as a cultural statement.

Musically too, *The Clash* is more sophisticated than originally perceived. Having unloaded their two most overtly voluminous and confrontational songs for their debut single, the group were now free to record those numbers that had real hooks, proper bridges, genuine choruses. That they downplayed any pop sensibility with vocal shouts, amplified feedback and atonal guitar solos failed to prevent the tracks standing the test of time as great *songs*, pure and simple.

Finally, and crucially, The Clash embraced variety. It's there in the thirteen Strummer-Jones compositions for those who have listened to *The Clash* often enough. But it's most pronounced in the six-minute rendition of Junior Murvin's 'Police And Thieves'. The group's audacious adaptation of this reggae number separated them from other punk groups who wouldn't dare to (or more likely, simply couldn't) play black music, and hinted at future musical evolution. The Clash, both the group and the album, refused to be confined to the sound of the white riot.

Terry Chimes, who refused a full time role due to philosophical differences, played drums on all 14 songs. He's credited, with more humour than malice, as Tory Crimes. Production is credited to Micky Foote. The unaccredited engineer was Simon Humphreys. CBS Records deserves credit for staying out of the studio, though that was not entirely altruistic: the album had barely been released before the label started trying to dictate proceedings. The American arm of CBS meanwhile, in a magnified display of myopia, 'passed' on the album. *The Clash* nonetheless seeped, and eventually flooded, into the States as an import, by which process it sold an unprecedented 100,000 copies. In the UK, *The Clash* was, for all its confrontational stance, a considerable commercial success, spending much of 1977 in the album charts, and peaking at number 12.

JANIE JONES

The opening song on *The Clash* features almost all the album's familiar ingredients: staccato guitars, lo-fi drums and bass, a chorus half-sung and half-shouted in three-person unison, and largely indiscernible lyrics. (On closer examination, the words glorify "rock'n'roll" and "getting stoned" from the perspective of a frustrated office employee whose sexual relief is to be found with the title character.) Mick Jones' phonetic harmony towards the end of the two-minute anthem is the first appearance of a particularly popular and enduring Clash trademark.

Jones had originally written 'Janie Jones' in the first person, on the number 31 bus from his Westbourne Grove home to Camden Town rehearsals, but Strummer balked at singing "I'm in love" with anyone. The perspective was switched to the third person – "He's in love with Janie Jones" - and the song's prominent placement as opening track suggests that the group recognised its atypical approach.

The real life Janie Jones was a British Madam who had been front page fodder back in 1973. But by the time of the song's release, The Clash were attracting such a young audience that many didn't understand the reference. In that sense, too, 'Janie Jones' is something of an anomaly on an album that is otherwise very much rooted in the social maelstrom of urban Britain, 1976-77.

REMOTE CONTROL

Written, primarily by Mick Jones, following the farcical Anarchy In The UK tour of December 1976. The Clash had set off with The Sex Pistols, The Damned and, from New York, The Heartbreakers, on a schedule of 19 shows intended to introduce the nation to some new street-wise rock'n'roll. On the eve of the tour, The Sex Pistols had their infamous expletive-ridden run-in with Bill Grundy on live British TV, which provoked media hysteria and encouraged local councils to ban almost all the concerts under the pathetic pretence of 'protecting' their constituents. The Sex Pistols barely played in Britain again.

But 'Remote Control' cast a wider net than the "civic hall", complaining also about the lack of options in London after the pubs shut at eleven each night, and throwing a veiled reference to the EMI board meeting after which that label dropped The Sex Pistols from its roster. That's on the occasions when the words can be heard: Joe Strummer and Mick Jones alternate vocals here, and prove that poor pronunciation was a band trait. Strummer defended the group's diction in an interview at time of the album's release, stating "Our music is like Jamaican stuff – if they can't hear it, they're not supposed to hear it. It's not for them if they can't understand it." 'Remote Control' is the only song on the album not to take any possessive perspective, which might explain its placement directly after 'Janie Jones'. From here on, all Strummer-Jones compositions on The Clash are sung in the first person.

Despite its sharp lyrics, 'Remote Control' betrays its relative youth with a hackneyed, glam-like opening riff, an uninspired guitar solo and tame drumming. That it was the softest song on the album naturally inspired CBS to release it as the album's second single, against the Clash's wishes and despite their belief that their contract granted them 'complete control.' The 'Remote Control' single (backed by a "live" rendition of 'London's Burning', in fact recorded for a promo film) was a commercial failure, partly because The Clash urged their fans not to buy it.

I'M SO BORED WITH THE U.S.A.

Originally titled 'I'm So Bored With You', Mick Jones' long-standing anti-love song was quickly turned into an anti-American rant when Joe Strummer joined the group. The lyrics are quite advanced for supposed anti-intellectuals, aiming barbs at military adventurism (Cambodia), Washington intrigue (Watergate) and cultural imperialism (Kojak). When The Clash embarked on a mutual love affair with America only a year after the album's release, they attempted to downplay the song's intent, though the lyrics were so direct there was little wriggle room. In reality, there was no need to apologise for directing some of their considerable anger in such an obvious direction, and American youth demonstrated equal ambivalence towards the USA by lapping up The Clash in those unprecedented import numbers. 'I'm So Bored' is driven by a sing-along chorus, constant bass notes and a succession of hard-hitting guitar riffs – a perfect punk anthem. Throughout the album, the rhythm guitars are "hard-panned" (one to the left speaker, one to the right); this is the first number on which the effect is clearly in evidence.

WHITE RIOT

A different mix than the single, thicker, more dense, with the vocal pushed up front for once, and notably absent the various sound effects. It all serves to render the song yet harder and more violent, the most uncompromising aural assault on the album.

HATE & WAR

Joe Strummer, 24 at time of The Clash's release, was old enough to remember the late Sixties hippy ethos of 'love and peace'. He inverted it for this statement of mid-Seventies reality, which he then painted on the back of his boiler suit jacket for emphasis. Many in The Clash audience, too young to make the hippy connection, simply understood 'Hate & War' as an accurate summation of the world in which they were living. Mick Jones ended up singing lead on one of the album's most musically commercial yet lyrically nihilistic numbers, wherein the singer stubbornly refuses to quit town and instead promises to meet violence with more of the same. The wonderful crack in Jones' voice as he reaches for the high notes offsets the unfortunate closing reference to getting "beat up by any Kebab Greek".

WHAT'S MY NAME

(Strummer-Jones-Levine)

The first Clash line-up temporarily included a third guitarist, Keith Levine (sometimes spelled Levene), who would later play in Johnny Rotten's post-Pistols band Public Image Limited. Levene's sole song-writing credit from his Clash period is 'What's

My Name', which he shares with Strummer and Jones. (Paul Simonon, who came up with the band name shortly after Strummer joined, was still struggling to learn bass as *The Clash* was recorded and therefore not granted any songwriting royalties.) The lyrics of 'What's My Name' can be seen either as fictional Clash self-glorification, or as an example of the narrative being projected beyond group experience to represent that of society's *real* outcast. Either way, with its propelling tom-tom drums, phonetic harmonies, use of the f-word and simplistic sing-along chorus, 'What's My Name' sounds like it was designed for the football terraces. In reality, and for all Simonon's dressed-up past as a Chelsea skinhead, there was almost no interaction between punk rockers and football fans in 1977.

DENY

A "love song" of sorts for punks, in which the narrator foregoes traditional romance and admiration to accuse his girlfriend of deceit and deception. There's a reference to the 100 Club, home base for punk gigs at time of the song's writing, and a none-too-subtle accusation of drug addiction. Vocal 'oohs' and guitar riffs reminiscent of Mick Jones' early Seventies heroes Mott The Hoople reveal The Clash's commercial influences, while Strummer's vocal performance is among his most urgent on the album. As pure a pop song as anything on *The Clash*.

LONDON'S BURNING

Written from the perspective of the 18th floor balcony at Wilmcote House, the tower block overlooking The Westway where Mick Jones lived with his grandmother during the early days of The Clash - but then actually composed by Strummer in near-silence in his own squat while his girlfriend, Palmolive of The Slits, slept in the same room. 'London's Burning' is often considered of a pair with 'White Riot': each song places itself in West London, cementing the group's association with the Notting Hill and Ladbroke Grove neighborhoods, and each expresses

dissatisfaction with these surroundings through shouted choruses, crude verses and the barest of melodies, lending itself to instant punk anthem status. Yet 'London's Burning' is also a companion to 'I'm So Bored With The U.S.A.', and as with that other song's vast target, The Clash were in fact using "boredom" to mask an obsession. Listen again and it's obvious that The Clash are genuinely *excited* by London's burning boredom. (Perhaps because, they grasped, they could now do something about it?) For all these reasons, 'London's Burning', though too musically simplistic to age well, would remain close to the group's heart, its title and imagery re-worked through much Clash and post-Clash material.

CAREER OPPORTUNITIES

For the three core members of The Clash, all of whom were all on the dole through much of 1975 and '76, unemployment was a matter of choice: they viewed the meagre weekly dole cheque as the natural successor to their art school grants. But as they discovered when they began playing in the north of England, employment was a matter of pride for many in the *real* working class, and the few low-end jobs on offer did nothing to inspire anyone's confidence in Government policies as jobless numbers rose to figures unknown since the Thirties. (And then, in the Eighties under Thatcher, rose beyond them.)

'Career Opportunities' then, is one of those songs in which the Clash project themselves through their own experiences, and then descend down the food chain until they're representing the desperate man at the very bottom of the pile. He shares with The Clash a refusal to take the crap jobs – despite a final recognition that he may have "no choice" – and it's this defiance that marks 'Career Opportunities' as such an emphatic, enduring protest anthem.

Bolstered by Mick Jones' power chords, which owe much here to Pete Townshend's rhythmic style of playing, Strummer's voice is mixed high, as if this one time he wants every words to be clearly understood. The dropped "t's" on the phrase "let'er bombs" and a shouted "Oi!" perhaps over-play his narrator's working class roots, but they may also be intended to down-play the song's commercial foundations. 'Career Opportunities' follows a classic pop pattern - intro, verse, chorus, verse, chorus, middle 8, verse, chorus, outro - all completed several seconds shy of two minutes. Its prominent placement as opening track on Side 2 provides confirmation of the group's own belief in the track.

CHEAT

Written during rehearsals for the album, 'Cheat' continued the nihilistic message of 'Hate & War'; taken together, the songs suggest The Clash's punk vision as inherently negative and violent. It's also worth noting that 'Cheat' encourages people to "learn how to lie" while, earlier in the album, the song 'Deny' berates a girlfriend for doing just that. But this is only a career contradiction for those who would assume every lyric to mirror Strummer and Jones' personal intent; from the perspective of the album's narrator, the dichotomy is part of his frustrating everyday life. A particularly strong middle eight leads into an extended back-to-basics Jones solo bolstered by phased rhythm guitars that continue into a rare fade-out.

PROTEX BLUE

Mick Jones sings lead on his only pre-Strummer song to make it to *The Clash* unaltered. As was the guitarist's particular punk skill, it's an anti-love song, concerning the era's predominant condom of the title. There's no sense of political correctness about using protection, just a typical male acknowledgement that "I didn't want to hold you". (And a final verse in which the Protex has become the singer's sexual accompaniment for the night.) Stereo separation of both guitars and drums, classic Clash vocal harmonies, and a guitar solo all of four seconds long do much to propel the song beyond the ordinary.

POLICE & THIEVES

(Murvin-Perry)

In 1976, with punk yet to make it onto record, Britain's only contemporary rebel music was Jamaican reggae. Given that both Simonon and Jones had roots in the heavily West Indian South London community around Brixton, and that all three members had moved into the similarly Caribbean-dominated Notting Hill, it's hardly surprising that the group lapped up reggae singles with almost as much enthusiasm as the local Rastafarians. One of them was Junior Murvin's 'Police & Thieves', co-written by that singer with producer Lee Perry, which became a big reggae hit that summer, peaking at the Notting Hill Carnival, where it gained extra credence given the subsequent riot. By the end of the year, The Clash were trying to turn a Bob Marley B-side, 'Dancing Shoes', into a punk song, but occasionally played 'Police & Thieves' for fun – and when Mick Jones had Strummer strike a power chord on the down beat, leaving himself free to accentuate the more familiar reggae upbeat, the group succeeded in creating their own distinct version. It was soon worked up into a six minute epic.

On record, the pared down rhythm affords the kick drum rare prominence; the group prove adept at instrumental drop-outs, as already practiced on their own material, and the deliberately thin Mick Jones solo, repeating the melody of the verse, is a moment of back-to-basics punk genius. It all builds through a lengthy second half with unmistakably white rage. "It was punk reggae, not white reggae," Strummer later observed. "We were bringing some of *our* roots to it." More than that, the recording served to drastically shift the mood of the album at the very moment it could have been written off as monochromatic; it formed a perfect counterpart to 'White Riot'; and it helped bring the length of the finished record well above thirty minutes. More than anything, it demonstrated that punk's love of reggae was more than mere lip service, and influenced a number of white groups, young and old, to try incorporating black music into their repertoire. The crossover success of The Police, the 2Tone label, and British reggae acts like Steel Pulse and Aswad can all be traced back to this song. The favour was returned almost immediately in highly appropriate fashion, when Lee Perry wrote and produced a B-side for the new Bob Marley single 'Jamming', called 'Punky Reggae Party'. It included the line "The Wailers will be there, The Damned, The Jam, The Clash..."

48 HOURS

Another song written close to completion of the album, '48 Hours' offers an echo to the last sharp British street movement, the mods of the Sixties, and their focus on the weekend. Again, The Clash were not singing from their own experience – as dole queue veterans, they hardly knew where the working week ended and the weekend started – but from that of their audience, the same frustrated lowly employee office employee of 'Janie Jones', screaming for his "48 Thrills". Unstated in the song except in its frantic pace (96 seconds, the shortest song on the album) is the fact that punks, like mods before them, lived largely on amphetamine, and that it was not uncommon for bands and audience alike to stay up for 48 hours straight. It seems appropriate then that Jones claims the song was written in just half an hour, and it's worth noting that, in December 1978, he claimed "I was so into speed, I don't even recall making the first album!"

GARAGELAND

The final song on *The Clash* was also the last to be written. Significantly, it's the first occasion whereby The Clash sing about themselves as a band. Soon enough, this would become their calling card, an unfortunate inversion of the "everyman" persona that dominates the debut album. At the time of 'Garageland' the self-mythologising had yet to fully take hold, so while the inspiration for the song was personal – a damning review in *NME* that concluded of The Clash, "They are the type of garage band who should be speedily

returned to the garage, preferably with the motor running," – the lyric was broadened to include every band that ever aspired to make a noise for the sheer gleeful hell of it. ("Twenty two singers! But one microphone!"). With the twin guitars (again hard-panned) drenched in reverb, and Jones contributing occasional harmonica, one of the album's strongest melodies finds Strummer referring to the group's major record deal but, crucially, without the details that would have rendered the song specific to The Clash alone. Instead, in the final verse Strummer venomously disassociates himself from "the rich". Those who found this amusing given his father's diplomatic status and his public schooling perhaps missed the point. No one has a say in how they are born, but everyone has a say in how they choose to live as adults. Strummer had long ago made that choice, and on 'Garageland' he appears to be inviting every other dissatisfied middle and upper-class kid to follow his lead, leave home and come join The Clash' revolution. Many would heed the call, and though some would come to question their leaders' own allegiance, as its own answer to the album's unstated but constantly suggested question "Which side are you on?", 'Garageland' provides *The Clash* with the perfect finale.

COMPLETE CONTROL/CITY OF THE DEAD

(UK single, September 1977)
The first recording featuring Nicky 'Topper' Headon on drums, 'Complete Control' is announced by one of the hardest-driving one-chord guitar riffs ever committed to vinyl. Louder, clearer, and more emphatically energetic than anything on *The Clash,* it barely lets up pace throughout. From a purely musical perspective, 'Complete Control' can be considered The Clash's finest punk rock statement.

But The Clash could never be separated from their lyrics, and 'Complete Control', words written entirely by Mick Jones for once, remains remarkable for a number of reasons. The similarity in title to the last single is explained in the opening line's unambiguous, unprecedented attack on the record company: "They said release 'Remote Control', we didn't want it on the label." There's another reference in the last verse, which rhymes the group's interpretation of their CBS contract – that they would be "artistically free" – with what they see as the record company's perspective: "let's make a lotsa mon-ee". (The term 'complete artistic control' is regularly written into recording contracts, and The Clash were not the first band to discover how difficult it can be to actually enforce.) The title is also a jibe at manager Bernie Rhodes who, just after the Anarchy tour, insisted the group give *him* "Complete Control". Finally, by spelling out part of the song title during the coda, The Clash acknowledged that they thought everything was a c-o-n.

Clash critics saw these complaints as confirming why the band should not have signed with CBS in the first place. And they had a point. Punk was meant to offer an alternative *to* the system, and by signing to a major record label that was part of an American-based multi-national media enterprise, The Clash were instead allowing themselves to be co-opted *by* the system. Independent labels like Stiff and Chiswick were beginning to make an impact at the time The Clash signed their controversial deal, and when The Buzzcocks released a self-financed EP around the same time as *The Clash* album, proving how easy it was to press up your own record, they helped launch an independent label boom that would render the next few years among the most creative in British music. (The Clash would later acknowledge this with the song 'Hitsville UK'.)

One of the intrinsic ironies of all the above is that, if The Clash had not taken the more troublesome path, they would never have been inspired to write 'Complete Control', revered by many astheir finest three minutes. And, considering the situation they were now in, they deserve enormous credit for not only recording a song that was openly critical of their record company, but for then

demanding the label release and promote it as proof of the band's creative freedom. That CBS went with the programme suggests that the label bore the group no malice – or that they were blithely familiar with the process of profiting from rebellion. The fact that 'Complete Control' barely scraped into the British top 30, at a time when other punk bands were starting to scale the top 10, should not be taken as evidence that the label then scuppered the single's progress: the recording was, simply, too furious for daytime radio.

Considering the song's voluminous punk energy, it's a surprise to see Lee Perry credited as producer. The madcap genius behind 'Police & Thieves' and 'Punky Reggae Party' had been lured into the studio by Bernie Rhodes, and The Clash leaped at the opportunity to further their "punk reggae" hybrid by also recording The Maytals' 'Pressure Drop' (from the Jamaican movie *The Harder They Come*). But though Perry impressed the band with his dub techniques, 'Pressure Drop' was shelved, and Mick Jones remixed 'Complete Control' on his own, returning the focus to the guitars. Earlier in 1977, Jones had told Tony Parsons of *NME*, "I don't believe in guitar heroes," but his superb solo halfway through the song (the first time he let rip on a Clash recording) proved too much for Strummer, who screams "You're my guitar hero" in good-natured recognition of this latest Clash contradiction, before name-checking himself as "Joe Public" during a furious ad-lib about punk's supposed fad status. All these references – to contracts, past singles and tours, and punk's trendiness with the media - should have rendered 'Complete Control' passé almost by time of release, but as Nick Hornby writes in his collection of essays, *31 Songs*, it continues to resonate decades later because "it still has something to say about naïvete and cynicism and artistic impotence."

'City Of The Dead' is notable for the inclusion of saxophones and keyboards, a brave step forward taken two steps back by the deliberate muffling of the words. What sounds like a familiar tale of urban disenchantment is in fact a continuation of the group's new tendency to sing about itself. There are allusions to The Clash being beaten up for the clothes they wear and a non-judgmental reference to Johnny Thunders ("New York Johnny") and his drug habits. As a sonic experiment and an interesting but imperfect song, it's an ideal B-side.

Complete Control: Available on TCUS, TS, TSOTC, COB, TEC.
City Of The Dead: Available on SBMC, COB.

CLASH CITY ROCKERS/JAIL GUITAR DOORS
(UK single, February 1978)

The new wave – as the record companies and media had re-named punk for mainstream marketing purposes – was largely driven by 7" singles, and none of the groups, not even The Clash, could afford to go more than a few months without releasing one. If 'Complete Control' confused those listeners who didn't know about the group's run-ins with their label and the police, 'Clash City Rockers' seemed more straightforward: an open invitation to join their gang. Yet the "rockers" referred to in the title were not street-fighters but a brand of hard-hitting reggae music. The Clash, it turned out, wanted only to move their listeners to a heavyweight bass sound.

The point may have come across better had the group backed it with a further exploration of reggae. But apart from a positive reference to Jamaican vocalist Prince Far-I, 'Clash City Rockers' eschews reggae references, building instead around a power chord riff reminiscent of the group's limited edition release 'Capital Radio', itself loosely based on The Who's 'I Can't Explain'. Laden with solos, a piano overdub, and an extended fade-out – on which Topper Headon lets loose for the first time - it was the longest Clash composition to date, at almost four minutes. It was rendered seven seconds shorter when Micky Foote, apparently at Bernie Rhodes' insistence, sped it up at the mastering, adding a further

sense of urgency. This understandably infuriated the band, who had only just sung about such back-handed matters on their last single. Foote would not work in the studio with the band again; Rhodes' days were also numbered. Released in February 1978, by which time The Sex Pistols had broken up and the 'new wave' bands were looking increasingly careerist, 'Clash City Rockers' again stood out for its direct delivery. Again, it was purchased only by the faithful hardcore.

'Jail Guitar Doors' was Mick Jones' tribute to three guitar heroes and their temporary incarceration: "Wayne" (Kramer, MC5), "Peter" (Green, Fleetwood Mac), and "Keith" (Richards, Rolling Stones). Peter Green was, as Jones sang, certified insane after trying to give his money away, a topic of relevance to The Clash and audience alike. Kramer and Richards, on the other hand, had been jailed for cocaine and heroin possession, respectively, and though Jones does not exactly come to praise them, nor does he bury them. (Jones was himself busted for cocaine possession on tour later in 1978.) The song title and melody were actually a lone hold-over from The 101ers; the simplistic blues riff in the middle betrays those roots.

Clash City Rockers. Vari-speeded 7" version available on TCUS, TSOTC, TS. Original, slower version available on, COB, TEC.
Jail Guitar Doors: Available on TCUS, COB, SBMC

(WHITE MAN) IN HAMMERSMITH PALAIS/THE PRISONER
(UK single, June 1978)

Last in the trio of singles that filled the lengthy gap between first and second Clash albums, '(White Man) In Hammersmith Palais' is nothing short of a masterpiece. A significant divergence in style from their previous punk anthems, it draws instead from the positive experience covering 'Police & Thieves'. In his inspirational three-part 1977 *NME* piece on The Clash (reprinted in the *Clash On*

Broadway booklet), Lester Bangs wrote that "Somewhere in (The Clash's) assimilation of reggae is the closest thing yet to the lost chord, the missing link between black music and white noise." He was talking, specifically, about '(White Man) In Hammersmith Palais', and its subsequent recording bore out Bangs' belief. It occupies a musical space entirely of its own construction.

Strummer's words are simultaneously his most slurred and most striking to date. They open with a roll call of contemporary Jamaican reggae artists (Dillinger, Delroy Wilson, Ken Boothe), referring to a concert Strummer attended at the venue of the song's title, where he was disappointed not just by the lack of "roots rock rebel" on stage, but by black boys snatching purses from white girls in the crowd. (Similar incidents had led to the oppressive police presence at the Notting Hill Carnival of their 'White Riot', though that was something The Clash never addressed.) Observations about this lack of solidarity between white and black youth segue into a firm denunciation of un-named punk rockers for wearing "Burton Suits" (that would be The Jam, who fell out with The Clash on the White Riot tour of 1977) and for "turning rebellion into money" (though the fact that CBS were pulling the same number on The Clash appeared to escape the band). A final reference to Adolf Hitler showing up in a limousine increases the song's sense of apocalyptic paranoia.

Throughout this frequently indiscernible but highly emotive diatribe (which opens with a short burst of guitar and a muffled count-in such as would normally be edited out of a single) the four musicians relish the opportunity to expand their musical horizons. Simonon and Headon quickly gel at the slower pace, an upright piano and woodblock add to the syncopation, and Mick Jones throws in an eerie new take on those otherwise familiar phonetic backing vocals, and as with 'Police & Thieves', a late crescendo leads to a distinctly punk finale. '(White Man)' is so dense and aggressive that, as with previous singles, it failed to

resonate with the wider public, but hardcore fans and music critics alike reacted with wild enthusiasm, voting it *NME*'s Single Of The Year – and the fact that it sounds so uniquely vivid 25 years later when so many other 'bigger' new wave hits of the era have been long forgotten is testament to The Clash's long-term vision.

Set against such a ground-breaking a-side, 'The Prisoner' is upbeat and lightweight, to the point of throwaway. But then that's what B-sides are for. Jones again takes lead vocals, and while the title can be seen as a continuation of the 'Jail Guitar Doors' theme, it's also a reference to the surreal sixties TV show of the same name. Paranoia was running rampant within the Clash camp at the time, and for good reason. The weight of expectation surrounding their ovderdue second album was threatening to bury them.

(White Man) In Hammersmith Palais:
Available on TCUS, TS, TSOTC, COB, TEC
The Prisoner: Available on SBMC, COB.

GIVE 'EM ENOUGH ROPE

(UK album, November 1978)

Many punk and new wave groups saw their movement as marking a return to the urgency of the Sixties, and hurriedly recorded second albums only a few months after equally rushed debuts. Not so The Clash. While their debut had been recorded free from outside interference, the interest sparked in America by the album's phenomenal import sales made certain that CBS demand a greater say in the follow-up. Sandy Pearlman, an American whose credits included Blue Öyster Cult and The Dictators, was recommended as producer, and The Clash, who could have refused, readily went along with the idea. They would later regret their acquiescence: the three non-album singles released in 1977 and '78 not only showed the group knew the right sound for themselves, but these songs might have helped steady the wavering quality of what became *Give 'Em Enough Rope* if, a) it was not strictly verboten for punk bands to include old singles on new albums, or b) the second album had not taken so long to get going.

Part of the delay was unavoidable: the start date was put back three months when Joe Strummer contracted Hepatitis B in early 1978, after swallowing the saliva of spitting fans on stage. But the actual process of recording, once it got under way at London's Basing Street Studios in May, was painstakingly laborious, the exact opposite of the speed-driven urgency that drove *The*

Clash. Pearlman favoured multiple takes and conventional working hours. The group took to spending the down time watching war movies.

After five weeks at Basing Street, Pearlman returned to America, and Strummer and Jones joined him, first at The Automatt in San Francisco, then at the Record Plant in New York, to add overdubs and oversee the mixes. (Simonon and Headon flew in for final mixes in New York.) Though not oblivious to accusations from British fans that they were selling out to America at first invitation, The Clash by now felt compelled to go with Pearlman's programme rather than let CBS authorise third party mixes. Still, internal frustration at their own helplessness was externally confirmed when they sacked Bernie Rhodes shortly before the album's release. As so often the case once a streetwise band moves up to the international market, and budgeting becomes more important than politicking, the group's original mover and prime propagandist was found lacking in key areas. One of them, it should be stated, was failing to take the lead and find a producer amenable to band, label *and* audience.

To the relief of all concerned, the finished album largely fulfilled expectations, at least through Side 1. But as *Give 'Em Enough Rope* sagged in the middle and then descended into rock cliché, fans and critics alike became all too aware of repetitive subject matter which, stripped to the song titles' core words, read like a tired tabloid headline: "Gun... Gang... Drug... War..." Even though some of these songs were written with tongue in cheek, it was hard not to conclude that The Clash were glorifying, perhaps even wallowing, in their outlaw status.

Give 'Em Enough Rope enjoyed considerable British success, peaking at number two in the busy pre-Christmas season, and served, as intended, in opening The Clash up to America (and vice versa). Given that The Clash bounced back quickly from the disheartening experience, *Give 'Em Enough Rope* can be viewed in hindsight less as a colossal disappointment and more as a temporary downturn.

SAFE EUROPEAN HOME

To use a metaphor relevant to its frequent subject matter, *Give 'Em Enough Rope* comes out with all guns blazing. On 'Safe European Home', the sound is both bigger and cleaner than *The Clash* and its subsequent singles, with guitars to the fore, and drums pronounced, yet it doesn't seem remotely compromised. Most notably, and perhaps reassuringly, Strummer remains largely unintelligible throughout.

The lyrics were, however, frequently and readily explained. At the start of 1978, Jones and Strummer had taken a working holiday in Jamaica, intending to write new songs in the reggae homeland. (Paul Simonon, the group's real reggae expert and the only one to have attended a London comprehensive school dominated by Jamaican immigrants, was livid at being left behind.) But the trip provided a serious reality check once the duo took to wandering the streets of Kingston, in full punk regalia, looking for their only contact, Lee Perry. Aware that their white skin was "an invitation to robbery", and unsuccessful in finding Perry, they holed up at their hotel, venturing into town only to watch movies (more for audience interaction than for what was on the screen) or to score weed. The whole experience is documented with admirable honesty on 'Safe European Home', the title reflecting the duo's desire to return to London's relative security.

The music of 'Safe European Home' confirms its lyrical inspiration only in the extended coda, with an off-beat guitar riff and Strummer's repeated lyrical observation that "Rudie can't fail" as Jones sings the title behind him. But as the drums come roaring back in, this can also be read as a final Clash statement on Jamaican music, and an acknowledgement that from here on – at least for the duration of *Give 'Em Enough Rope* – The Clash are ready to leave "punk reggae" behind and embrace, instead, safe western rock'n'roll.

ENGLISH CIVIL WAR

(Traditional, arranged Strummer-Jones)

Appropriately enough for an album that tried to blend English punk rock with American Adult Oriented Rock, 'English Civil War' was a Strummer-Jones rewrite of the traditional American civil war song 'When Johnny Comes Marching Home'. The lyrics portray some kind of fascist takeover in the group's home country, a subject of genuine concern during the punk years. (The election of Margaret Thatcher as Prime Minister in May 1979, setting the Conservative Party on 18 consecutive years of Government, both forestalled and fulfilled that threat.) But it's hard to ascertain Strummer's moral position, which renders the song less of a protest or warning and more of a fictional glorification.

Musically, 'English Civil War' moves with enough confidence and precision that it's over in just two and a half minutes, by far the shortest track on the album. All guitars are played by Mick Jones, including an extensive but sharp solo that starts just a minute in. As with the similarly-placed 'Remote Control' on the debut album, 'English Civil War' was to be the album's second single, this time *with* the group's consent.

TOMMY GUN

Topper Headon's double-delivered machine-gun drum rolls announce *Rope*'s first single and one of its undisputed highlights. 'Tommy Gun' maintains The Clash's punk fury, while upgrading the sound to an approximation of heavy metal, yet somehow making the combination palatable to daytime radio – no small achievement for a song that fetishises terrorists. Joe Strummer, always the most politically involved member of The Clash, had found himself swept up in revolutionary zeal towards the end of a decade in which armed groups like the IRA, the PLO, Red Brigades, and Red Army Faction all graced the newspaper front pages for their violent activities. On 'Tommy Gun', Strummer asks whether they're doing it for the cause, or the celebrity, but in questioning the glamorisation of terrorists, he comes perilously close to glamorising them himself. (The album cover, on which vultures feed on a cowboy as Chinese communists come marching across the plains, further reflects this fascination with revolutionary chic, though it was perhaps also intended to offset the album's otherwise obvious American capitalist connotations.)

As Strummer becomes increasingly worked up about his subjects, Mick Jones offers a typically inspired one-note solo and Nicky Headon revels in a rare centre-stage performance, ending the song as violently as he starts it, this time accompanied by a burst of feedback. Considering the song's chaotic arrangement, provocative lyrics, and lack of a conventional chorus, it may seem surprising that 'Tommy Gun' succeeded where previous Clash singles had failed, scaling the British Top 20 at the peak of the Christmas 1978 single-buying season. But this achievement was surely aided by the generous publicity surrounding the album, suggesting that the preceding three non-album singles, all of which were relative commercial disappointments, would surely have fared better under similar circumstances.

JULIE'S BEEN WORKING FOR THE DRUG SQUAD

A welcome change of pace, introducing a jazzy rhythm and blues sound such as would soon become a regular part of The Clash repertoire. With piano parts overdubbed in New York by that city's veteran New York bluesmen Gloves Grover and Al Fields, 'Julie' owes a musical debt to America. But its lyrics are firmly entrenched in the story of an undercover British police operation which infiltrated and took down an LSD production facility. Strummer sings cheerfully of traditionally straight-laced policemen and women tripping on acid to maintain their cover, but he also references the lengthy prison sentences handed down to those busted, a likely result of Operation Julie's considerable mainstream media coverage. It's the second song in a row in which Strummer is singing not from personal experience, but from newspaper cuttings, suggesting an uncertainty of intent such as was never the case with *The Clash*. The song's effortlessly enjoyable arrangement overrides such qualms.

LAST GANG IN TOWN

At over five minutes, 'Last Gang In Town' is the longest Strummer-Jones composition to date, built around an uninspired blues guitar riff that offers no respite to the simplistically structured verses other than a chorus which descends into the minor key. In a very British take on the enduring imagery of *West Side Story*, Strummer sings soulfully of "Quiffs", "Spikes", "Rastafari" and "skinheads" facing off against each other on the mean streets of London. But absent the conclusions that rendered '(White Man) In Hammersmith Palais' such a remarkable observation on youth culture, 'Last Gang In Town' would in time come to be seen as a self-glorifying reference to The Clash themselves. Mick Jones attempts to rescue the plodding rhythm with some creative guitar work throughout the last minute, but he can't prevent the song providing a disappointing conclusion to *Rope's* first side.

GUNS ON THE ROOF

(Strummer-Jones-Headon-Simonon)

The Clash had been embracing their own mythology in song since 'Garageland', but 'Guns On The Roof' brought the concept close to caricature. In March 1978, Topper Headon and Paul Simonon, along with Mick Jones' best friend Robin Crocker (see 'Stay Free') and two of Headon's mates from his hometown of Dover, took an air rifle on the roof of The Clash's Camden Town rehearsal space. There they started shooting at nearby pigeons – valuable racing pigeons, as they found out to their cost – but given their proximity to the railway tracks leading into London's main line stations, the gunfire aroused suspicions of a terrorist attack. The five were quickly confronted by police toting *real* weaponry, arrested, imprisoned for the night and, three months later, fined a measly £30 each – though also forced to pay £700 in damages to the racing pigeons' owner.

Rather than apologising for the embarrassing incident, The Clash named a song for it, taking collective writing credit as if the farce gave them rebel status equivalent to the anti-heroes of 'Tommy Gun'. Strummer, who wasn't party to the shooting and arrest, uses the roof as a take-off point for a wider lyric about global gun-running and terrorism, but never criticises the rhythm section's overgrown playground activities.

Dubious subject matter can always be masked by an inspired performance, and 'Guns On The Roof' is nothing if not energetic. But it relies on almost precisely the same chord structure as 'Clash City Rockers' and 'Capital Radio' before it, doing little to convince even the most hardened Clash fan that the group weren't running short on ideas.

DRUG-STABBING TIME

Segued from 'Guns On The Roof' via Mick Jones' descending guitar outro, 'Drug-Stabbing Time' combines classic Clash energy with a meaty sax overdub (courtesy of New Yorker Stan Bronstein), some prominently mixed cowbells and a grand Mick Jones guitar line two minutes in. But just as 'Guns On The Roof' was the second song on *Rope* to reference firearms in its title, so this was the second to include the word 'drug'. And while 'Julie's Been Working For The Drug Squad' was clearly a piece of reportage, 'Drug-Stabbing Time' seemed far more ambiguous. The first Clash album had frequently demanded that the audience choose which side it was on; with songs like 'Tommy Gun' and 'Drug-Stabbing Time', *Give 'Em Enough Rope* now invited the same question of The Clash.

STAY FREE

Clearly influenced by Mott The Hoople, 'Stay Free' is essentially a solo Mick Jones song about his teenage friendship with Robin Crocker. A renowned

hard case who doubled as a pro-Clash journalist for *Zigzag* under the name Robin Banks, Crocker also went on tour with The Clash, achieving notoriety for beating on a young fan in writer Lester Bangs' presence (provoking a negative conclusion to an otherwise celebratory piece in *NME* in 1977), punching Sandy Pearlman to the floor the first time the producer attempted to come backstage, and being part of the quintet arrested for those "guns on the roof". Jones paints his former Strand Grammar School partner in rather more affectionate colours, reminiscing fondly about "having fun" in the classroom, and "dancing down Streatham" before Jones, as narrator, opts to focus on guitar, while his (crucially) un-named friend's career in crime escalates towards the almost inevitable "three years in Brixton" (prison). Jones appears to have learned from songwriting icons like Bruce Springsteen and Ian Hunter that local details can give a song universal appeal; 'Stay Free' is firmly placed in South London yet would invoke similar nostalgic memories amongst Clash fans across the globe.

With Strummer nowhere to be heard, 'Stay Free' is the least cluttered song on the album. Keyboard overdubs courtesy of The Rumour's Bob Andrews can be picked out in the background, while the rhythm section luxuriates in its rare breathing space. (Several of Simonon's bass lines were re-recorded once the sessions moved to America; the playing on 'Stay Free' is certainly among the most adept on the album.) The fade-out guitar solo is Jones at his best – overtly competent but not overly flashy, it seems intended as a homage to his glam rock heroes.

CHEAPSKATES

Sadly, having been reined in for much of the album, Jones' lead guitar now runs riot through *Rope*'s last two songs. The effect is particularly incongruous on 'Cheapskates', given that the song is intended as an attack on rock clichés. In marked contrast to Jones, Strummer affects a tuneless roar akin to Sham 69's Jimmy Pursey, deadening the relatively sprightly chorus as he claims prior employment as a "washer-up" and insists that one Clash member has "never read a book", as if a badge of honour. The final verse denounces media suppositions that a successful group like The Clash should be drawn to "model girls" and cocaine, despite considerable evidence that that's precisely what was happening to them.

To be fair, Strummer found himself in an intensely difficult situation in 1978. He had spent the last few years living in squats, had contracted Hepatitis from spitting fans, counted his worldly possessions in plastic bags and, other Clash members notwithstanding, personally disdained rock star behaviour. All of which meant he took a public hiding when discovered living in a fancy house off Regent's Park - even though he was only a temporary guest of Clash sleeve designer and Habitat family scion Sebastian Conran, occupying just one unfurnished room. The criticism provoked him to move back into a 'real' squat and write 'Cheapskates'; in retrospect both actions could be seen as a mistake, but Strummer's most endearing and enduring character trait was a determination to act honestly to the moment.

ALL THE YOUNG PUNKS (NEW BOOTS AND CONTRACTS)

Yet another self-referential song to end an album dominated by them. The title – and its opening guitar lick – is a clear reference to Mott The Hoople's 1972 anthem 'All The Young Dudes'; the "new boots and contracts" sub-title is a direct throw-back to the second verse of 'Garageland', which itself had closed out the first album. But where 'Garageland' was full of optimistic defiance, 'All The Young Punks' sounds disappointed, even jaded, from the Ian Hunter-esque lyrics and their strained delivery through the tired band performance. Sandy Pearlman seems determined to compensate for these defects by thickening up the production, but it ends up sounding muddied instead; the album fades to the sound of Mick Jones wailing away obliviously at the top end of his guitar, and Strummer mumbling an ad-lib, having unconvincingly declared band life better than that working in a factory. Overall, it's almost

impossible not to share the group's sense of defeat. For the last year, as the musical revolution fizzled out in front of them, and their heroes' second album took on the weight of the Second Coming, Clash fans had been grappling with the question, Is Punk Dead? The Clash appear to end *Give 'Em Enough Rope* by answering in the resounding and depressing affirmative.

THE COST OF LIVING EP
(UK, May 1979)

Following the exasperating transatlantic studio sessions for *Give 'Em Enough Rope*, The Clash were determined to prove that they could still record and release songs with speed and enthusiasm. Under the pretext of tightening up live recordings for the semi-documentary movie *Rude Boy*, they entered London's Wessex Studios in January 1979 and quickly worked up a four-song EP of old and new songs. The name was a reference to the media catch-phrase of the inflationary Seventies, one the group found amusing when used in isolation. They laughed a little less when the record company priced what was meant to be a value-packaged release for full EP price. Production credits were shared between The Clash and chief Wessex engineer Bill Price. It marked the start of a lengthy working relationship.

I FOUGHT THE LAW
(S. Curtis)

The 1966 hit by the Bobby Fuller Four was Mick and Joe's favorite single on the Automatt studio jukebox in San Francisco; Strummer played it incessantly as a means by which to learn the piano. He and Mick subsequently brought it to the Clash rhythm section, and once Topper beefed it up with some notable drum rolls, it was introduced into the live set in late 1978. The studio version is as keenly enthusiastic as it is patently commercial, especially in the latter choruses, where the guitars drop out to emphasise the hand-claps and percussion.

The decision to release 'I Fought The Law' as a British A-side was not without risk. The group's two previous studio cover versions had both been Jamaican reggae songs

('Pressure Drop' having finally made it onto the B-side of 'English Civil War'), a music considered partly British by nature of the nation's massive West Indian immigrant population. But 'I Fought The Law' was unmistakably American in structure, tone, and delivery, and following hot on the heels of *Give 'Em Enough Rope*, it offered further ammunition to those who accused the group of switching attention to the world's biggest music market. Such suppositions seemed confirmed when the song, recorded just before The Clash's first visit to the States in support of *Give 'Em Enough Rope*, became the group's first ever American single.

The lyrics, too, took on added weight when sung by The Clash, and it was hard not to see them as yet further self-glorification in light of the members' various arrests both on and off tour over the previous year.

GROOVY TIMES

Another notably commercial production, full of harmonicas and acoustic guitars, 'Groovy Times' had been demoed for *Give 'Em Enough Rope*, but passed over in favour of harder, denser material. Not that 'Groovy Times' was frivolous: the lyrics, delivered with newly determined clarity by Strummer, refer to fences round the football terraces, trigger-happy policemen and a stubbornly optimistic media that chooses to ignore such dark omens. It may have been mere coincidence that *The Cost Of Living* was released the week after Margaret Thatcher was elected Prime Minister, but given how much of Britain's conservative media saw her victory as a return to "groovy times" (albeit by a less groovy term), the timing seemed particularly pertinent.

GATES OF THE WEST

A Mick Jones composition that dated back to pre-Strummer days under the pre-punk title 'Ooh, Baby, Ooh (It's Not Over)', then rewritten as 'Rusted Chrome' and recorded at Basing Street with Sandy Pearlman. In New York, Jones reworked and then sang the lyrics to reflect his journey from "Camden Town Station to 44th and 8th" in yet another autobiographical, Mott The Hoople-like attempt to make every Clash adventure worthy of a musical monument. While such a lyric may have fitted perfectly on *Give 'Em Enough Rope*, it's notable that The Clash mix has greater clarity than almost anything on the Pearlman-produced album.

CAPITAL RADIO TWO

In April 1977, as a marketing ploy, *NME* offered readers an interview with Tony Parsons as front cover material, and a free 'EP' via a mail-in voucher printed in the paper. The EP's lead track was a vituperative attack on London's lone 'independent' music radio station, 'Capital Radio'; like 'Complete Control', it was a monumental rock'n'roll example of biting the hand that feeds - except The Clash had determined that Capital catered only for housewives and advertisers, meaning the band had nothing to lose by assailing the station. References to Nazi propagandist Dr. Goebbels and the naming of individual station DJs nonetheless rendered 'Capital Radio' extreme even by the standards of punk.

Of course, along the way, the *NME* single became a much-prized rarity, and while The Clash couldn't release the original recording without nullifying its promised 'limited edition' status, they *could* re-record it in the hope of bringing the black market price down. 'Capital Radio Two' opens with acoustic guitar, rushes through a louder, harder version of the original (improved significantly by Headon's drumming), then breaks down with a Springsteen-esque verbal adlib by Strummer about what *might* get them played on the radio – at which the group launches into a punked-up disco funk. As an inadvertent statement of future intent, this brief jam provides the EP with a remarkably prescient finale.

I FOUGHT THE LAW:
Available on TCUS, TS, TSOTC, TEC
GROOVY TIMES/GATES OF THE WEST:
Available on SBMC, COB.
CAPITAL RADIO TWO: Available on SBMC

THE CLASH (US)

(USA only, July 1979)

Clash City Rockers/I'm So Bored With The U.S.A./Remote Control/Complete Control/White Riot/(White Man) In Hammersmith Palais/London's Burning/I Fought The Law/Janie Jones/Career Opportunities/What's My Name/Hate & War/Police & Thieves/Jail Guitar Doors/Garageland

Seven months after *Give 'Em Enough Rope*, and following the spectacular six-figure import sales of *The Clash*, Epic Records (one of CBS's two American imprints) finally succumbed to public demand and released the first Clash album. To cover their backs, they reconfigured it with the group's subsequent non-album A-sides – leaping over *Give 'Em Enough Rope* to include 'I Fought The Law' - and one B-side, 'Jail Guitar Doors'. To make room for these tracks, four songs from the original album were dropped. The result only led to further Stateside confusion about what really constituted the band's first album, and the American edition of *The Clash* is best viewed in hindsight as an early Best Of. Still, allowing how hard it must have been for many American fans to pick up the various 7" singles on import, the move made sense, and though the sequencing has little rhyme or reason, it's hard to dispute the collective impact of the fifteen songs. Both 'Clash City Rockers' (speeded-up) and 'White Riot' (with sound effects) are the 7" versions.

LONDON CALLING

(UK album, December 1979, USA January 1980)

The Clash's finest moment was born out of their darkest hour. The group had reached a precipitously low ebb by early 1979. There was the enervating process of recording *Give 'Em Enough Rope*, and the group's own doubts with the finished album, despite its commercial success. There were awkward battles with the American record company over lack of financing for the first tour, and then the reality check of that nation's industry norms (and occasional audience indifference) once they finally played across the Atlantic. Most frustrating were the ongoing legal battles with former manager Bernie Rhodes, who had frozen their assets and forced them to vacate their long-standing rehearsal space in Camden Town. Penniless and homeless, it was time to either put up or break up, and given that there was no talk of the latter, The Clash found themselves a permanent new rehearsal space, Vanilla, on Caulfield Causton Street in Pimlico, just north of the River Thames, and focused all their energies in the only direction they really knew: the music.

Retreating into the security of their own solidarity, the group found their spirits lifted immediately and immeasurably, and were soon writing and demo-recording their most varied music to date. "Desperation – I'd recommend it," said Strummer at the end of the year. "The problem seemed to relax us, the feeling that nothing really mattered any more."

Strummer was so enamored by the group's back-to-basics approach, he suggested they record the album straight to tape at Vanilla; without studio costs, he figured, it could be released for a bargain price. CBS didn't see it that way, but after hearing the new songs (*The Vanilla Tapes* were finally released as part of a 25th Anniversary deluxe edition in 2004, and are reviewed here in the Commemorative Editions section), label bigwigs Mo Oberstein and Muff Winwood agreed to fund sessions at Wessex, the group's preferred multi-track studio and, this time round, to the group's own choice of producer: Guy Stevens.

As the man who assembled Mott The Hoople and produced the Hereford band's first four albums, Stevens had been Mick Jones' teenage studio idol. That admiration had been dampened, according to Marcus Gray's Clash biography *The Last Gang In Town*, when Stevens was brought in to administer a mid-Seventies Mick Jones band only to edge the future Clash guitarist out of the line-up - and again, when hired to produce Clash demos for Polydor in 1976, only to show up drunk. Jones was either proving phenomenally patient with the maverick producer - or thinking far ahead, knowing that he'd be earning himself significant studio input by giving the troubled Stevens another chance.

Stories of Stevens' production techniques have become the stuff of legend. Engineer Bill Price, in the *Westway To The World* documentary, claims Stevens installed "the maximum emotion in a record… by a process of direct psychic injection." The producer's manic enthusiasm certainly came as a relief after Pearlman's clinical perfectionism, and even his habit of throwing chairs and ladders around the studio to increase the performers' energy didn't faze a band that had long thrived on aggression. But Stevens couldn't slow down, and as his alcoholism affected first his performance and then his attendance, Mick Jones duly slid into the producer's chair to oversee the overdubs. In public, The Clash were never anything but generous about Stevens' input, awarding him full production credit; Bill Price and Jeremy Green were credited as Chief and Second Engineers, respectively.

The Clash were determined to release every song they recorded at Wessex, and equally adamant to keep the retail price down. CBS balked at a low-cost double album and so the band, as their legend has it, initially convinced the label to include a free bonus 12" single instead, then delivered no less than nine extra songs to fill it to capacity. "It was our first real victory over CBS," declared Strummer, proudly, that December.

It was a victory for everyone, and it absolutely hinged on the deliberate inclusion of so many songs at such a low price. The Clash understood now from experience that one man's B-side was another's Desert Island Disc, and that their audience would readily forgive the occasional diversion into unfamiliar territory as long as there were enough solid recordings to excuse the experiments. Stripped to a single disc, those most solid songs suitably tightened up, *London Calling* could have been faultless, but it would not have enabled the album's *real* calling: its sense of adventure. For where other punk bands had either broken up, embraced the pop mainstream, descended into cliché or, in the case of The Jam (the best of The Clash's 1977 rivals), perfected a very *British* outlook, The Clash now stepped fearlessly beyond their punk roots to embrace rockabilly, jazz, reggae, rhythm and blues, calypso, rocksteady, disco, and funk, while never neglecting their rock roots. That the finished recordings on *London Calling* often lacked polish was very much part of their appeal: The Clash had also learned from their previous two albums that they were better at selling emotion than precision, and *London Calling* exudes a certain spiritual ecstasy, the communicable joy of a group stretching effortlessly beyond its previously perceived possibilities.

London Calling provided The Clash with their biggest hit single in the UK, and gradually rose into the top 30 of the American album charts, a significant achievement for a British so-called punk band. That success was seen by some as confirmation of the album's original intent for, despite its title, *London Calling* borrowed heavily from American music and mythology. Even the cover, a Pennie Smith shot of Paul Simonon smashing his bass at New York's Palladium, was designed to look like the debut Elvis Presley album sleeve.

Certainly, *London Calling*'s influence on America cannot be underestimated. At the end of the decade, the writers of America's leading music magazine, *Rolling Stone*, voted it the #1 Album of the Eighties. But then, early the following Century, both *Q* and *The Observer* magazines placed it in the Top 5 British Albums of all time, too. (In the UK, its earlier release date means it's considered the last great album of the Seventies.) Such enduring, international praise helps cement *London Calling*'s standing as a classic rock'n'roll album. Make that a double.

 ### LONDON CALLING

Opening song, title track, and as first single, both the biggest UK hit The Clash would have through the course of their working career (it made #11) and their first successful attempt at a promo video (filmed in the rain at Battersea Pier by Don Letts). 'London Calling' is a four-to-the-floor rocker such as audiences may have hoped for, but there's a brightness to the sound absent the group's previous recordings: the guitars are strident but restrained, the bass firmly stated, the drums supremely confident. Strummer appears to be consciously pronouncing his words (ironic, given that this album is the first to include lyrics on the inner sleeves – designed by *NME* cartoonist Ray Lowry) as he returns to the apocalyptic vision of 'English Civil War'. London is now a capital where "war is declared" and "battle come down," one where "nuclear error" appears to have brought on a new "ice age". Anticipating renewed suggestions that he might be glamorising his subject matter, he insists the audience "don't look to us" and instead makes a metaphorical dive into the oncoming flood. His meaning may be more muffled than his pronunciation, for once, but the song immediately became – and remained - a rock radio staple, one of the group's most readily identifiable anthems.

BRAND NEW CADILLAC
(Vince Taylor)
It was Paul Simonon, rather than the group's presumed rock'n'roll fanatic Joe Strummer, who brought this Vince Taylor B-side from 1959 to the band's attention. Taylor was a British-born, American-raised maverick who came of age at the birth of rock'n'roll, then returned to the UK to try and make his fortune; David Bowie has credited him as an inspiration for Ziggy Stardust. The Clash rendition of 'Brand New Cadillac' is astoundingly forceful, a reverb-drenched guitar riff opening up from the right speaker, a fierce second rhythm guitar then stabbing in on the left, and a piercing lead riding roughshod over the top as Strummer wails the words with wild delight. Much more abrasive than their cover of 'I Fought The Law', it's an early warning that *London Calling* will go where it wants to. If it's true that this is the first take of the first song Guy Stevens heard when he walked into Wessex, it would confirm the producer's gut instinct – and the band's own, for hiring him.

JIMMY JAZZ
The Brand New Cadillac sets off across the deep American south, dropping The Clash off somewhere round New Orleans, where they kick back, slow the pace, pull out an acoustic guitar to accompany the electric ones, invite in a brass section (The Irish Horns) for the first time on the album, and sing of a fictional character in trouble with the police for chopping off people's heads. More meaningless glorification of fictional violence? Perhaps. But the relaxed mood affords The Clash breathing space and renders such accusations a little mean. All

the same, Strummer seems aware of the group's shifting base, spelling out the word jazz with both American ("zee zee") and British ("zed zed") pronunciations of the alphabet's final letter.

HATEFUL
The Clash broke with touring tradition when they hired rock'n'roll pioneer Bo Diddley as opening act for their first short tour of the States in February 1979. It was inevitable then that the Bo Diddley beat would end up somewhere on *London Calling*, and here it is, providing the backing for a raw, up-tempo number sung from the perspective of a drug addict, largely about his "hateful" dealer. Mick Jones interjects Strummer's verses by throwing his words back at him as snappy questions – classic drug paranoia tactics. Jones' guitar work, especially the opening drone-like riff, is inspired, and the overall performance is among the tightest on the album.

RUDIE CAN'T FAIL
Set to a title previously referenced on 'Safe European Home', 'Rudie Can't Fail' leans towards the rock-steady ska sound that swept Britain in mid-1979 via the 2Tone label. The Clash were hardly jumping the bandwagon: their punk-reggae hybrid had been a vital influence on 2Tone bands and audience alike, and they had taken the label's founders, The Specials (then called The Coventry Automatics), on tour in 1978, back when Bernie Rhodes managed both bands. Delivered for the soundtrack of their semi-documentary movie (promptly titled *Rude Boy* in return), it's widely assumed that 'Rudie Can't Fail' is about that film's central character Ray Gange, but Strummer later claimed that the band themselves were also drinking "(Special) brew for breakfast" through much of '78. Regardless, with its sassy brass section and Calypso rhythms, and vocals shared by Strummer and Jones – "Sing Michael, sing!" urges Joe in the first few seconds - it's a cheerful tribute to the eternal underdog, and the group's first incursion into an up-tempo Caribbean sound.

SPANISH BOMBS

Jones and Strummer share vocals again in an intelligently crafted song that draws a triangular link between the following: the British volunteers who fought for the Republic in the Spanish Civil War of 1939, the British tourists flying in to the Costa Brava "on a DC10 tonight", and the ongoing bombing campaign of those same tourist beaches by the Basque separatists ETA. The singers don't try and find sense in all this; they're merely serving as reporters. Set to a restrained, melodic arrangement complete with acoustic guitars and the first notable performance by Blockheads' keyboard player Mickey Gallagher, 'Spanish Bombs' represents a considerable musical and lyrical step forward for The Clash. The chorus line, sung in Spanish, adds to the sense of a fast-maturing group.

THE RIGHT PROFILE

Guy Stevens brought a biography of the American actor Montgomery Clift to the studio and urged the band to read it. They went one further and wrote 'The Right Profile', a brass-accompanied, piano-inflected, jazzy rock jam that positively pulsates with the group's new-found enthusiasm. The Damned, who were recording in the next door studio at Wessex, later voiced the opinion that original backing tracks to *London Calling* were a total shambles. 'The Right Profile' would seem an obvious target for the rival punk band's ire, given how the rough arrangement is bolstered by layers of overdubs, but the looseness comes as relief after the almost robotic performances on *Give 'Em Enough Rope*. The title stems from a car accident in which Clift suffered permanent facial injuries, after which he was only filmed in "right profile".

LOST IN THE SUPERMARKET

Mick Jones sings lead with the kind of frailty that renders the lyrics, all suburban alienation, especially potent. Yet it was Strummer who wrote them, after finding himself bemused by the bright lights of the all-night grocery near his new hi-rise home on the King's Road. Such symbiotic interaction between the two writers and vocalists is one of *London Calling*'s star attractions, the living embodiment of the Lennon-McCartney myth. Topper's deft touch on the hi-hats and tom-toms, a pumping bass melody and a twanging guitar all serve to enhance the lyrics' sense of nostalgia.

CLAMPDOWN

Tucked away near the end of Side 2 (deliberately?) is *London Calling*'s most blatant rock anthem and yet its most potent protest song. Inspired by the near-meltdown at the Three Mile Island nuclear power station in Harrisburg, Pennsylvania, 'Clampdown' includes fascism, censorship and brutality of all stripes in its sights. The group not only state their own refusal to work for the clampdown, but urge listeners to "kick over the wall/cause governments to fall". As a call to revolt, 'Clampdown' is on a different lyrical plane than 'White Riot' from just three years earlier, and as it gained airplay on American rock radio, thanks to judicious use of feedback, widespread power chords, four-to-the-floor drumming and a call-and-response vocal, The Clash may have felt that they'd successfully subverted the system from within. Jones steps in to sing the middle eight underneath Gallagher's effective organ overdub, while the falsettos on the coda owe more than a nod to The Rolling Stones.

THE GUNS OF BRIXTON

(Paul Simonon)

Simonon's first songwriting credit is set to an archetypal reggae bass line, one he'd been working up for weeks before telling the group he had lyrics to accompany it. Strummer then encouraged the bassist to sing them himself, and Simonon just about pulls it off as he drawls a tale of defiant gangsters straight out of *The Harder They Come*, shifting the location from Kingston, Jamaica, to his own childhood neighborhood of Brixton. It's difficult not to hear the song as payback to Strummer and Jones for leaving Simonon behind on their own songwriting trip to Jamaica: certainly, it's closer to "roots rock reggae" than anything the group had yet recorded. While there were those who decried the lyrics as yet *more* self-serving glorification of violence (and Simonon, who loved guns, could hardly argue the fact), 'The Guns Of Brixton' has proven extraordinarily enduring. Simonon's bass line was lifted for the Beats International British number one single 'Dub Be Good To Me' in 1990, after which the track was remixed as an official Clash 12" single ('Return To Brixton'). It has been covered in styles ranging from rockabilly to bossa nova and has been sampled by acts as far afield as California's Cypress Hill.

WRONG 'EM BOYO
(C. Alphanso)
Another cover version suggested by Simonon. The Rulers' 1967 recording for the Trojan label, originally entitled 'Wrong Embryo', joins 'Rudie Can't Fail' as a brass-heavy thumbs-up to Britain's new obsession with ska. Strummer, having noted the reference to 'Stagger Lee', opens the song (and Side 3 of the vinyl double album) with a one-verse rendition from the Lloyd Price original of that name. America, Jamaica and England all in one song – a prime example of *London Calling*'s global ambitions.

DEATH OR GLORY
A mid-tempo rocker, with acoustic guitar forming a pad under the lead and rhythm electrics, and a singalong chorus that helps make it one of *London Calling*'s most effortlessly enjoyable numbers. The title suggests so much (more) Clash self-mythologising, but the lyrics – among the most poetic on the album - soon reveal the opposite intent. They're most astute on the second verse, which opens by referring to the prospective rock'n'roll star who "tell(s) us he'll die before he's sold" (Joe Strummer circa 1977) and concludes, with brazen imagery, "that he who fucks nuns will later join the Church" (The Clash, 1979?). For an album that finds The Clash triumphantly leaving their musical punk roots behind, but struggling to escape the movement's ethics, it's a key statement, both of intent and guilt.

KOKA KOLA
The middle eight's reference to cocaine is superfluous: it's apparent throughout as to which type of coke the Clash are referring. But the admittedly razor-sharp put-downs about executives taking their "top up long before the happy hour" can't disguise a certain hypocrisy; The Clash were hardly innocents when it came to the touring musician's favorite pick-me-up. The observation has been made that *London Calling* deliberate includes tracks that might normally have been relegated to B-sides; 'Koka Kola', the shortest of the 19 songs, would likely top most such lists.

THE CARD CHEAT
As another song about fated gamblers, and coming so soon after 'Wrong 'Em Boyo', there's a suggestion that The Clash have been reduced to feeding off their own cover versions, but the lyric is in fact an astute reworking of a scene from the Bergman movie *The Seventh Seal*. Musically, meanwhile, there's an unexpected Phil Spector influence: dramatic piano chords, booming drums, thick wall of brass and, less surprisingly, given that Mott The Hoople were also heavily influenced by Spector, Mick Jones singing lead at the top of his natural range. Whether it was Jones or Guy Stevens who suggested copying the Spector knack of recording each instrument twice to build the necessary Wall of Sound, it works.

LOVER'S ROCK
Named for a popular style of reggae, but performed as a relatively straight pop song, 'Lover's Rock' finds The Clash finally singing about romance, almost three years after their debut album. Not surprisingly given the lack of practice, the group are found lacking in finesse, and though Mick Jones sings a falsetto harmony and contributes a rather trite solo in an attempt to bolster Strummer's noble intent (lyrics based on *The Tao Of Love And Sex*), the song never reaches climax. The Clash had, until now, always been a boys' band, and 'Lover's Rock' did little to suggest that might change in the immediate future.

FOUR HORSEMEN

A solid Clash song, which with its title refrain, clever chord changes, syncopated drum rolls and wailing guitars, would have made more sense beefed up further by Sandy Pearlman and placed on *Give 'Em Enough Rope*. Indeed, the lyric is a throwback to the previous album's self-mythologising, and though Strummer has often insisted that The Clash were no more the 'Four Horsemen' than 'The Last Gang In Town', the fact remains that a smart lyricist anticipates audience reactions and writes accordingly.

I'M NOT DOWN

A straight segue into a Mick Jones vocal of defiance in the face of "depression" – an honest document of his break-up with The Slits' Viv Albertine. The music, however, reflecting the song's message of resilience, is resolutely upbeat, borrowing guitar licks from Motown, melodies from Seventies pop and ending up sounding like no-one but The Clash. Given more time in the studio – the original recordings came from a mere five-week session - one imagines 'I'm Not Down' sounding even stronger, and it's hard not to conclude from this and preceding Jones songs that there's a romantic pop songwriter lurking underneath the rock'n'roll punk.

REVOLUTION ROCK

(J. Edwards-D. Ray)

Another straight segue, this time into the album's third and last cover version, The Clash again embracing the reggae that had proven such a vital component of their early sound. As with 'Rudie Can't Fail' and 'Wrong 'Em Boyo', The Clash treat the Danny Ray song with more of a rocksteady/bluebeat bent, the upbeat rhythm serving to emphasise the optimistic message. (Beyond a call to "smash up your seats", there's no real call to revolution.) Given breathing space, the track moves into a rhythm breakdown that rivals The Beat's 'Ranking Full Stop' for frenetic precision, after which it's bolstered again by brass, then stripped down for Mickey Gallagher's Hammond organ

to shine in the background as Strummer calls out credits to the various instruments in one of the album's most exuberant vocal performances. As the album's intended finale, 'Revolution Rock' is a joyous celebration of the whole recording process.

TRAIN IN VAIN (STAND BY ME)

Fans have come to accept 'Train In Vain' as *London Calling*'s last song, but first-time listeners had no such expectations. Stickers on the British release announced '18 Track Double Album' at a single album price of '£5'; there was no mention of a nineteenth song on either the sleeve or the label. Only the most astute observer, counting the tracks on the vinyl itself, would have noticed that Side 4 had one more song than it was meant to. The biggest shock about 'Train In Vain', however (originally also referred to as 'Stand By Me' for its chorus line), was the music. Over a taut Jackson 5-at-the-disco rhythm, Mick Jones fulfilled his song-writing destiny (as hinted at on 'I'm Not Down') sooner rather than later, double-tracking a lead vocal that was, indisputably, of romantic nature. (Sample lyric: "I can't be happy without you around.") Coming at the end of an album that constantly explored new sounds, 'Train In Vain' confirmed The Clash as a band capable of anything.

For some Clash fans who'd bought in to the group in '76/ '77 for the political punk rock, 'Train In Vain' proved a break-up song of a different sort. But as word spread of the 'bonus' cut's funky rhythm, instantly memorable melody and sheer joie de vivre, many new fans came on board to make up the numbers. The American label Epic instinctively released 'Train In Vain' as a single (regardless of the group's considerations), whereupon it rose rapidly into the top 40, a first American hit single for The Clash on only their second attempt. Epic then stickered *London Calling* to advertise the presence of a 'Hit Single' that otherwise remained stubbornly unlisted. ('Train In Vain' was added to the back cover track listing only with the 1999 CD re-issue, by which time the drum track had been sampled by Garbage for *their* international hit, 'Stupid Girl'.)

Initial audience instinct that 'Train In Vain' went unlisted because it marked such a drastic musical departure for The Clash is apparently incorrect. According to then publicist Kosmo Vinyl's notes on the *Clash On Broadway* box set, The Clash were asked to contribute an exclusive cut for an *NME* flexi-disc, and Mick Jones showed up at Wessex with his new funky love song which was, supposedly, learned, recorded and mixed in a day. (That part may be apocryphal: there was enough time to bring back Mickey Gallagher and the Irish Horns.) Either *NME*'s publishers postponed the flexi at the last moment, as Vinyl wrote, or, as Mick Jones claimed in 2004, 'We thought "This is a bit too good to give away to the NME."' Regardless, the song was added to *London Calling* at the eleventh hour –with sleeves, stickers and labels already at the printers, and no time left for any credit other than a reference on the run-off groove. Kosmo Vinyl claims that if he'd known there were any unused tracks sitting around (a cover of Booker T. & The M.G.'s 'Time Is Tight' later showed up), he wouldn't have asked for a new song. But then The Clash would have been without an American hit, and their *opus magnus* minus its *grand finale.*

 BANKROBBER/ROCKER'S GALORE
(UK single, August 1980)

Rather than release more songs from *London Calling* – not that there was any shortage of candidates – The Clash entered 1980 planning an ongoing series of brand new British singles, hoping that a continuous presence in their home country's charts would nullify accusations that they'd switched focus to the States. In the meantime, they took Jamaican DJ, toaster and producer Mikey Dread on a UK tour with them through January and February; a creative partnership blossomed quickly and The Clash invited Dread to produce the first of the year's singles.

'Bankrobber' had originally been written in a rocksteady/ska vein, but the group had handled that style twice on *London Calling*, and with their cover of the contemporary Willie Williams song 'Armagideon Time' for the 'London Calling' B-side, had again proved that, when the mood took them, they were the most authentic white reggae group going. Recorded during a day off in Manchester, 'Bankrobber' was duly slowed to a dub tempo, with a melodic piano line (courtesy of Mickey Gallagher) and haunting backing vocals augmenting a rock-solid rhythm section and Mikey Dread's inimitable sound effects. Strummer wailed a fictional tale about a bank-robbing dad "who never hurt nobody" which, as the ultimate Clash romanticisation of the gangster, was so preposterous that there was nothing to do but laugh it off and sing along. Though possibly strange to anyone unaccustomed to real reggae, 'Bankrobber' had the distinctive sound of an instant classic.

Incredulously, CBS boss Mo Oberstein refused to release it. The Clash often claim they were told it "sounded like David Bowie backwards" (which perhaps it does, and why would that not be of interest?) and twenty years later, talking to Don Letts for the *Westway To The World* documentary, Strummer still sounded hurt by the decision. "It was hard enough making the records without having to deal with somebody who… didn't have the grace to go, 'Okay, well maybe you've got something here.'" Undeterred, The Clash secured 'Bankrobber''s release for a B-side in Holland, and watched with quiet satisfaction as import copies sold rapidly in UK shops. Chagrined, CBS finally released 'Bankrobber' as an A-side in August – seven months after it had been recorded - at which it rocketed up the British charts to peak at number 12.

Almost a full year later, former support group The Specials finally slowed down their own ska beat to a 'Bankrobber'-like groove and had a British number one spot with 'Ghost Town'. The Clash were vindicated, then, both over the short and long term, but yet again at considerable cost: the record company's initial rejection rendered the group's Singles Campaign stillborn. The initial intent of catering to the British fan base now took a back seat as the group headed to New York to record their new album.

For 'Rockers Galore…UK Tour', Mikey Dread toasts over the 'Bankrobber' backing track about touring with The Clash. This archetypal slice of vocal reggae, which could easily have passed as Jamaican in origin, showed up on the Dutch single B-sides along with 'Bankrobber', but was never released in America and is absent from all commercially released Clash albums. Its only CD appearance is on the limited edition album of the same name , Rockers Galore, issued by Sony in 1999 to promote the newly mastered back catalogue and live album. The Rockers Galore album intersperses tracks from different Clash albums with old promotional interviews in which the band members explain their origins and their development up until 1981.

SANDINISTA!

(UK album, December 1980, USA January 1981)

Is it possible to have too much of a good thing? *Sandinista!* would seem to suggest so. The Clash reacted to the success of *London Calling*, a double album sold at single album price, by expanding its value-for-money concept to the next (il)logical step: a triple vinyl album for (in the UK, at least) single album price. Yet, given the speed at which they recorded and mixed the music, quality was bound to take a backseat to quantity, and the 36-song, six-sided *Sandinista!* quickly revealed itself on release as a sprawling, confused, overly ambitious, frequently self-indulgent and yet occasionally brilliant work of madness.

The credits confirm the chaos. *Sandinista!* was recorded at five studios in three countries; both production and songwriting were, for the first time, collectively attributed to The Clash; the set was 'recorded and mixed' by Bill Price; Mikey Dread, who shared a couple of songwriting credits, received an additional listing for 'Version Mix'. The musical net was cast yet wider than *London Calling,* with disco, hip-hop, soul, jazz, gospel, country, folk, rock, skiffle, calypso and, especially, reggae, all in the mix.

Indeed, *Sandinista!* was so vast it found room for four dub versions, four cover versions (including one old Clash song), a couple of revamps of its own new offerings, a

duet between Mick Jones and his girlfriend, the appearance of other guest musicians ranging from gospel choirs to the keyboard player's kids, and even a previously released single by an associated artist! The Clash were not unaware that they were selling some form of musical insanity: Strummer remarked on the album's release that, faced with American interviewers' request to explain the group's new musical direction, he instead wondered, "Can't they see we're a bunch of idiots who'll do whatever we wanna do?"

Such a frivolous attitude should have been welcomed in a group who, with *London Calling*, had found themselves one calculated step away from international super-stardom. But it proved painfully hard for fans to sift the occasionally glimpsed gold from the surrounding muck (an appropriate term given the frequently opaque production) and many of those who bought *Sandinista!*, even at intended discount price, complained that they would have far preferred, this time out, one single album of fully focused, carefully crafted, properly produced and clearly mixed songs.

Yet *Sandinista!*'s over-indulgence and under-production is also its triple triumph. It stands as a unique document of a great group at its peak of creativity, allowing the audience in on its inspiration, and demonstrating itself as unafraid of embracing different musical genres as of tackling global political subject matter. Though largely out of step with its contemporary cultural climate, whole sections of the triple album have weathered well the winds of time, especially the successful interactions with the nascent New York hip-hop scene and the quality of its reggae arrangements. Inadvertently, *Sandinista!* also offered a firm taste of what was to come with the compact disc; for most of the Nineties, artists felt compelled to fill every available moment of the new 80-minute discs, leading to ever more lengthy albums (and unlike The Clash, an ever greater distance of time between them). In return – or perhaps, in revenge - consumers exercised the right to their remote control, skipping over tracks they disliked from the freedom of their sofa. *Sandinista!*, available these days as a lengthy double CD, continues to invite such instant editing even from the most avid fans. The group don't appear to have ever expected otherwise.

Perhaps the most generous way to look at *Sandinista!* with the benefit of over twenty years hindsight is as a compilation of the group's intended Singles Campaign. Or better yet, as a collection of EPs. Had the Clash been encouraged to release new recordings as they happened, what we now know as *Sandinista!* could have provided a series of excellent radio-friendly A-sides, backed by no shortage of inspired dub versions, interesting cover choices, brave experimental compositions and occasionally willful disasters such as fans are willing to excuse under the right circumstances.

But that's not how it happened, and at the time, *Sandinista!* received a well-rounded critical mauling, often for reasons that have not stood up as well as the music itself. British fans proved steadfastly uninterested in the value-for-money concept, leaving *Sandinista!* with the worst UK sales and chart record of any Clash album. American fans, though not treated to the same discount pricing and having only just been issued the B-sides collection *Black Market Clash*, bought *Sandinista!* in enough numbers for it to follow *London Calling* into that country's Top 30. That disparity in trans-Atlantic popularity can be taken as evidence either of blind American loyalty, or of insular British small-mindedness. Either way, *Sandinista!* remains, in every sense, a proud statement of Internationalism.

THE MAGNIFICENT SEVEN

'The Magnificent Seven' is directly and unapologetically influenced by The Sugarhill Gang's 'Rapper's Delight'. Despite that pioneering rap single's phenomenal sales in late 1979/early 1980, the sound of spoken rhyme over instrumental disco was written off by many industry insiders as a temporary novelty. It proved

instead to be the birth of a black music form to rival rock'n'roll, which makes it appropriate that *Sandinista!*'s opening cut should also be the album's most enduring song. Enormous credit is due to The Clash for their continued instinct in picking up on, and then improving upon, current musical trends.

New York City provided the song's cultural inspiration. The Clash decamped to that city's Power Station and Electric Ladyland studios for a month after a brief American tour in March 1980, whereupon Mick Jones immersed himself in the city's nascent hip-hop culture. The looped, liquid disco-funk bass-line was supplied not by Paul Simonon – he had committed himself to a doomed movie role back in the UK - but by The Blockheads' Norman Watt-Roy, who flew in for the sessions with his band-mate Mickey Gallagher. (A quick listen to Ian Dury & The Blockheads' 'Reasons To Be Cheerful, Part 3' will confirm Watt-Roy's suitability for this particular role.)

But it was Joe Strummer who claimed the song. The Clash front man had always been better at shouting than singing, and the new style of 'rap' allowed him a middle ground where he could speak his lyrics to excellent effect. 'The Magnificent Seven' is a delicious rant against the monotony of work, Strummer proving himself adept at rap's tendency to cultural details, quickly expanding his points of reference beyond hip-hop's New York City home into the global political arena, thereby setting *Sandinista!*'s theme. Considering that 'The Magnificent Seven' predated Blondie's hip-hop crossover hit 'Rapture' by several months - and the first 'reality rap' single, Grandmaster Flash & The Furious Five's 'The Message', by a full two years - it's a remarkably prescient recording. But then it's an example of something often forgotten about The Clash: that they were music *fans*, first and foremost, and a fan's enthusiasm often stands the test of time much better than clinical calculation.

An edited version of 'The Magnificent Seven' was released as the second American single from *Sandinista!*, accompanied by an instrumental remix which promptly exploded on black New York radio stations, much to the group's delight. In the UK, it was saved for a third single, in which format it failed to win over new fans.

A final note about the title. 'The Magnificent Seven' was a pseudonym for the gang of Clash musicians and side-kicks who would join support act Mikey Dread on stage, dancing in disguise; they took that name, of course, from the famous 1960 western, such movies being the dominant genre for urban youth in Jamaica. In America, kung-fu flicks played a similarly pivotal role with urban youth, and early hip-hop acts often named themselves in homage of outlaw heroes: *Grandmaster* Flash, Kurtis *Blow*, The Treacherous Three and The Furious Five. That The Clash had already claimed for themselves The Magnificent Seven may explain why an incursion into hip-hop was inevitable – and why it would sound so natural.

HITSVILLE U.K.

From New York, home of hip-hop and disco, to Detroit, home of Motown Records and known, in that label's heyday, as Hitsville USA. The Motown influence is apparent in the rhythm track, with the syncopated bass line and vibrant off-beat snare/tambourine reminiscent of a dozen Supremes/Vandellas' hits. Mick Jones and his girlfriend Ellen Foley (backing singer to Meat Loaf at the time) are no Marvin Gaye and Tammi Terrell, however, preferring to sing the melody together, rather than swapping lines as per the classic Motown duet. And it doesn't work: where 'The Magnificent Seven' marks the ongoing development of a contemporary new sound, 'Hitsville U.K.' seems like a desperate imitation of retro soul, succeeding only if its original intent was to be unrecognisable as The Clash.

Lyrically, the song pays tribute to Britain's thriving post-punk independent record label scene, name-checking leading labels Fast, Rough Trade, Factory and Small Wonder. This can be read either as an apology by The Clash for not going the independent route

themselves back in 1977, or as their patronising a scene they were never willing to engage in. Either way, the group felt strongly enough about 'Hitsville U.K.' to release it as the first American, and second British, single from the album. It was an enormous commercial disappointment in each nation.

JUNCO PARTNER

(Robert Ellen)

An old 101ers stage favorite, revived for *Sandinista!* after Joe Strummer's 101ers-era violin-playing friend Tymon Dogg was invited into the recording process. 'Junco Partner' was recorded in Kingston, Jamaica's legendary Channel 1 studio, which explains why it has a heavier dub feel than anything yet to appear on a Clash album. (With Mikey Dread on board, The Clash figured they could finally record in the home of their reggae heroes, but the Kingston sessions were quickly abandoned after local Dread Rastas demanded financial recompense from the white rock band. 'Junco Partner' was the only song to make it onto tape.) The relatively simple rhythm track is aided by Mickey Gallagher's keyboards and Dogg's violin, over which Strummer affects a particularly tuneless Jamaican vocal style as he rants about junkies. The Clash had sung about drugs with something close to an addict's regularity, but the topic moved closer to their heart as Topper Headon developed a debilitating predilection for heroin: his drumming through *Sandinista!* is notably weaker than on *London Calling*. Sadly, if 'Junco Partner' was intended as a message to Headon, it went unheeded. Nonetheless, its order within the sequencing seems more than mere coincidence.

IVAN MEETS G.I. JOE

Nicky Headon's lone lead vocal for The Clash is set to an arrangement that reflects the drummer's love of soul and disco, with a Stax-like brass section and another funky bass line courtesy of Watt-Roy. Given the questionable quality of the other Clash members' singing, it seems unfair to bury Headon's passable vocal so far back in the mix, raising to prominence instead sound effects from inter-galactic arcade games as a street-wise commentary on the cold war battle of the song's title. But in this sense, The Clash were again ahead of the times: a year later, 'Planet Rock' would emerge from the New York hip-hop/dance club scene as the first electro anthem, unleashing a long-lasting craze for the musical sounds of the arcade games.

As (accidental?) compensation, the lyrics are elaborated upon into cartoon form in the accompanying Armagideon Times lyric sheet by artist Steve Bell, performing the same job as did Ray Lowry with *London Calling*. 'Ivan Meets G.I. Joe' imagines representatives of the Super Powers competing on the dance floor, with requisite military metaphors.

THE LEADER

Musically, an innocent good-time rockabilly cut with four verses and sing-along choruses all completed well short of two minutes; lyrically, a sly comment on the British tabloid newspapers' penchant for exposing political sex scandals, and the British population's complicity for lapping them up in the Sunday papers. It says something for *Sandinista!*'s range thus far that 'The Leader' is the first song to sound anything like The Clash of old.

SOMETHING ABOUT ENGLAND

Mick Jones opens by repeating the frequently heard opinion of old Englishmen at the time, that the country would be better off without the immigrants, while Mickey Gallagher tinkles nostalgically on the piano in the background. Strummer then takes over to summarise the old man's *real* life experience: two world wars, a depression, and decades of poverty and class struggle. It's an eloquent, non-judgmental observation on how those low in society tend to blame those yet lower for their problems – as opposed to attacking those in power up above. Yet the lyrics are so weighty that they struggle to form a tune and when they do, it's let down by singalong music hall choruses and the overly obvious use of brass bands.

REBEL WALTZ

True to title, a three-four rhythm for a fighter's lament. Though The Clash had long embraced the rebels of reggae lore, and some of *Sandinista!* was about rebellion in the form of revolution, the most obvious connotation for Strummer's vocal is the Confederate rebels of the American Civil War. It's hard not to see this lone Clash encroachment into the waltz tempo, accompanied by an appropriate harpsichord keyboard setting, as further romanticisation of the battle-field.

LOOK HERE
(Mose Alison)

The Clash scat-sing the opening verse of this Mose Alison song before launching into an impressively jazzy arrangement. If it doesn't sound like The Clash, then that's because, to a large extent, it is not: Mickey Gallagher's piano and vibes are the dominant instruments, followed closely by jazz bass lines so fluid they could only be the work of Norman Watt-Roy. (Paul Simonon, who returned to the New York sessions to overdub some bass lines and, once back at Wessex in London, play others from scratch, had improved over the years, but not to this extent.) Topper Headon, who grew up playing jazz more than he did rock music, shows that he hasn't forgotten any tricks, but he prefers a laid back performance as opposed to taking the lead. The lyrics fit well into Clash subject matter, insisting the listener make use of their life before it's too late.

THE CROOKED BEAT

A return visit to 'The Guns Of Brixton', down to South London reference, dub bass line and Paul Simonon's distinctly tuneless but nonetheless endearing vocal performance. Sadly, it's not a patch on its predecessor from *London Calling* and suggests that Simonon was having trouble expanding his songwriting. But then the band performance, which sounds incomplete rather than simply sparse, hardly helps. 'The Crooked Beat' gives way to the album's first dub version, Mikey Dread's distinct dancehall cry announcing his presence at the controls. For all the popularity of 2Tone ska and The Police's pop reggae, dub reggae was still an underground taste in the UK, and barely even identified in the USA, which renders its frequent appearance on *Sandinista!* a brave move for a supposedly white rock band. In this case, it works: 'The Crooked Dub' is far more interesting than the track from which it derives. It concludes with Mikey Dread announcing the next cut with the reggae descriptor "Murder!"

SOMEBODY GOT MURDERED

About as close to a Clash song as anything yet to grace *Sandinista!*, and a Mick Jones vocal at that, 'Somebody Got Murdered' was written after music producer Jack Nitzche asked the group to write a "heavy rock number" for the new Al Pacino movie, *Cruising*. Strummer based the lyric on the murder of the attendant at his Chelsea high-rise's underground car park, Jones wrote the melody, and the song was swiftly recorded. Mick's vocals, always more gentle than Joe's, and mixed far back in this case, lends the song a sympathetic, pleading edge, in contrast to Topper's dog, Battersea, who can be heard barking in the background. The movie commission petered away, leaving *Sandinista!,* thankfully, with one of its more conventional Clash songs.

ONE MORE TIME/ONE MORE DUB

Another reggae song, again followed by – and this time attributed - a dub version. (Reggae 12" singles routinely include a dub version appended to the original.) Strummer's lyrics of life in the American ghetto are accompanied by an archetypal reggae bass line and the same sort of simple upright piano playing that rendered 'Bankrobber' so effective. Though it has the casual approach of a jam session, 'One More Time' sounds whole where 'The Crooked Beat' seemed incomplete; the subsequent dub version is a textbook example of the style, breaking down the original track to individual instruments, building them back up with effects, popping

vocals in and out while keeping the beat bubbling throughout before finally ending vinyl Side 2 in a cloud of what is surely marijuana smoke.

LIGHTNING STRIKES (NOT ONCE BUT TWICE)

The opening track for the second vinyl album is as an obvious attempt to replicate 'The Magnificent Seven'. Musically, it falls short: The rhythm is less precise, the funk never quite gets going and as with too much of *Sandinista!*, it sounds more like a jam than a complete composition. Crucially for a new musical form that placed emphasis on the spoken word, Strummer's rap is inexcusably buried back in the mix. Still, the words, what one can hear of them (or what one can read from the lyric sheet's white-on-black handwriting) are up there with 'The Magnificent Seven'; delivered with a combination of street vernacular and tourist's wonder, they form a loving tribute to New York City in all its chaotic glory.

At this point in time – mid-1980 - the New York music scene was embarking on a golden period of inter-racial, inter-borough, cross-cultural collaboration, which means The Clash were viewed not as invading imperialists but as welcome party-crashers. The Clash, in turn, were eager to bring a British outlook to the new sound, much as they had when they recorded 'Police & Thieves', hence the references to London – including the good old Westway and Ladbroke Grove – in the final verse.

UP IN HEAVEN (NOT ONLY HERE)

The overlap into a similarly titled song is deliberate: within seconds of Strummer name-checking The Clash's home city, Mick Jones is singing about "the towers of London". This was previously inhabited territory for The Clash, but as Mick still spent time with his gran at Wilmcote House, he was well positioned to revisit the "reality estates" both in person and in song. His lyrics are amongst the better observations about this regrettable part of the British post-war social fabric, and they hold up well against a final verse by deceased protest singer Phil Ochs. Again, it's a shame the vocals are placed low in the mix, frequently drenched in reverb. While the song has a fine melody and skilled guitar work by Jones, it is, like many of the tracks on *Sandinista!*, far too long, wandering around aimlessly for ninety seconds longer than its ideal three-minute cut-off.

CORNER SOUL

To a gentle reggae beat, accompanied by soulful female backing singers and brass strains, Strummer asks, "Is the music calling for a river of blood?" References to Ladbroke "Grove" leave little doubt that the music in question is that of the Notting Hill Carnival. (Since the events of August 1976 that inspired 'White Riot', the Carnival had become an annual flash point between black youth and the police.) But an event that took place during a break in recording *Sandinista!* suggests another inspiration for the song. Performing in Hamburg, the group were confronted by punk squatters who considered The Clash to be sell-outs and unleashed violence within the hall. Strummer hit a trouble-maker in the crowd with his Telecaster, opening up a river of blood on the man's head, and was briefly arrested after the show. He later declared himself frustrated by his actions, realising he had become "controlled" by violence. 'Corner Soul', then, as well as being an unusual musical direction for The Clash, is the sound of a street fighter growing up, maturing, and searching for a new path.

LET'S GO CRAZY

Any lingering doubts whether 'Corner Soul' was referring to the Notting Hill Carnival were dispelled in the first few seconds of 'Let's Go Crazy', in which reggae singer Ansil Collins is heard, presumably via a radio interview, calling for "peace in the Carnival and love". The Clash then embark on a calypso rhythm for the first time in their career - complete with steel drums - as Mick Jones leads a choral backing vocal and Strummer takes up a

syncopated spoken lead that expresses the various forces at work on Carnival Day: the police presence, the physical and emotive power of the sound systems, the effects of "ganja", and the lasting hurt of 400 years of slavery. The initial meaning of 'Lets Go Crazy' would appear to be as purely cathartic release of joy, but by the end of the song, Strummer's immersed in the Carnival's crazed violence. Perhaps the music *is* calling "for a river of blood", after all.

IF MUSIC COULD TALK

(Clash/Dread)

Staying with the Caribbean beat and the influence of music, The Clash augment a semi-acoustic reggae rhythm with an appropriately jazzy saxophone floating over the top, as Strummer riffs, beat poet stream-of-consciousness style, two different vocals – one in each channel. There are references to Buddy Holly, Clash touring partner Joe Ely, and Errol Flynn, but Strummer seems less concerned with unraveling the mystery of the title than suggesting the sounds that music makes. To the extent that the song is deliberately unfocused, it's a success.

THE SOUND OF SINNERS

To an ebullient gospel melody and a deeply intoned repetition of the words "judgement day", Strummer raises his voice high (literally as well as metaphorically) and describes his search for "that great jazz note that destroyed the walls of Jericho". Clash fans paid more attention to a chorus line which suggested the front man had found Jesus, and in interviews at the time, Strummer admitted to "getting kinda religious". But given the late-song voice-over by a white-sounding preacher passing the collection plate, it's obvious that Strummer had yet to be sold on organised religion. And the title 'The Sound Of Sinners' could as easily be taken as a wry reference to any new song by The Clash. (*Sandinista!* originally credited the song as 'The Sound Of *The* Sinners'; the 1999 CD re-issue dropped the second definitive article, perhaps by error.)

The initial intent for each side of *Sandinista!* vinyl to tell its own story is, sadly, lost in translation to CD. But Side 3's carefully segued journey from New York to London, its exploration of music's power to incite and heal, and its embrace of several different forms of black music, shows that more thought went into *Sandinista!* that some critics claimed. And as 'The Sound Of Sinners' rounds out the first of *Sandinista!*'s two compact discs, it at least allows for the pause that was also intended to follow 'Something About England' and 'One More Dub'.

POLICE ON MY BACK
(Eddy Grant)

It says something for *Sandinista!*'s experimental approach that the song which sounds most like The Clash is a cover version. 'Police On My Back', by Eddy Grant's late sixties band The Equals, was a Clash tour bus favourite, and the group used it to ease into recording sessions at New York's Power Station. Punctuated by a piercing high-pitched guitar riff courtesy of Mick Jones, and sung in unison by Jones and Strummer, 'Police On My Back' is a four-square rock anthem, the most clearly mixed, radio-friendly track on the whole triple album. Naturally, it was never released as a single. If it's a truism that you can tell a group by their covers, then following on from 'Police & Thieves' and 'I Fought The Law', 'Police On My Back' demonstrates that The Clash had yet to tire of their outlaw obsession.

MIDNIGHT LOG
Set to a casual rockabilly rhythm, Strummer sings in relatively abstract terms of otherwise familiar Clash demons: employment (on the night shift), police operations, and the cooking of the books at multi-corporations. But the rockabilly pulse works better on 'The Leader', and the lyrics (and melody) lack the necessary hook to raise 'Midnight Log' above its surrounding cuts.

THE EQUALISER
A return to dub reggae. 'The Equaliser' is a powerful rallying cry for equal rights and equal pay on the job, with The Clash, in determined 'Clampdown' mode, urging workers everywhere to "Put down the tools" till "half and half is equalised". (With the royalties for their double and treble albums, The Clash were doing otherwise in their own relationship with CBS – offering ever greater productivity while allowing their income to be negotiated downwards.) As with 'Junco Partner', the reggae vibe is bolstered by Tymon Dogg's violin. 'The Equaliser' appears to have little of Mikey Dread's usually identifiable input, mixing its dub inflections into the song itself, rather than being separated into two separate recordings.

THE CALL UP
Of all the mysteries surrounding *Sandinista!*, the biggest must be the decision to release 'The Call Up' as first UK single. For a group that was undergoing constant criticism from home nation fans for focusing on America, the choice of a song that included a Marine marching chant and which was clearly aimed at American listeners (if in typically anti-Establishment mode, urging them "not to heed the call up") defied all common sense. Perhaps the vaguely ska rhythm seemed suitably *au courant* to British tastes, maybe the melody sounded soft enough for daytime radio, or else the guest appearance by Richard Hell's guitarist Ivan Julien was deemed of some cult cachet; any which way, it was a commercial disaster, the group's lowest chart placing since 'Remote Control'.

On the notes to the *Clash On Broadway* box set, Mick Jones claimed that 'The Call Up' was written in opposition to the draft, in which case it was a decade too late: President Nixon had scrapped the controversial system of conscription back in 1973. Then again, rumours of its return are common in American politics.

Separated from its context as a British single, removed of its ludicrous marching chants and treated just as an album track, 'The Call Up' is pleasantly emotive, Jones and Strummer sharing vocals, while a glockenspiel melody vies for instrumental center stage alongside a restrained guitar riff. But it's also ridiculously long, at five and a half minutes, and anyone who sees the video of The Clash performing in army fatigues will struggle to take 'The Call Up' as seriously as The Clash had intended.

WASHINGTON BULLETS

Again it becomes clear how much thought was put into *Sandinista!*'s sequencing, as 'Washington Bullets' follows 'The Call Up' in both musical tone and lyrical attitude. The track responsible for *Sandinista!*'s title and in many ways the album's cornerstone, 'Washington Bullets' is one of the most informed – and informative – lyrics The Clash ever mustered. (Strummer wrote most of his lyrics in a 'Spliff Bunker' built out of flight cases and intended to scare hangers-on from crowding the control room.) After referring to a 14 year old getting shot in Kingston while The Clash were in Jamaica trying to record, it quickly expands into an inspired attack on empire, expansionism and military power of all stripes. America – those Washington Bullets – is criticised for its role in the Chilean coup and the aborted Bay Of Pigs invasion of Cuba. There then follows a celebration of the recent overthrow of the Nicaraguan dictator Anastasio Somoza, especially the fact that "America" – i.e., the USA – had this time not interfered. Recognising that not all global ills stem from Washington, Strummer points the finger at Russia for invading Afghanistan, China for interfering in Tibet, and Britain for the unspecific former Empire hell of it. The verses are interloped by choral naming of the Nicaraguan revolutionary movement: *Sandinista!*

The Clash themselves were unfamiliar with the Sandinistas until a politically motivated friend from San Francisco turned them on during the March 1980 tour. The Clash's conversion to the cause was typically total: they not only named the album for the revolutionaries (at Mick Jones' suggestion) but convinced the British arm of CBS (though notably not the American) to release it with the catalogue number FSLN1, the initials standing for Frente Sandinista de Liberación Nacional.

Fortunately, the music of 'Washington Bullets' lives up to its weighty subject matter. As with its *London Calling* antecedent, 'Spanish Bombs', the rhythm has a Hispanic lilt appropriate to the geography, with steel drums imitating South American marimbas. And as on several other *Sandinista!* cuts, the lyrics and their melody are greatly improved by having Jones and Strummer frequently sing in unison. Mickey Gallagher's organ swells proudly toward the song's conclusion.

An important footnote: Ronald Reagan was elected President of the USA around the time the *Sandinista!* album was released, and he determined to quell the Nicaraguan revolution before it inspired other Central American nations to similar left-wing uprisings. Those Washington Bullets were sent back down south in the guise of funding for the Nicaraguan Rebels – the Contras. The Sandinistas were sufficiently hampered by economic embargoes and guerilla warfare that many Nicaraguan citizens turned against them, and at the end of the Eighties, voted them out of office. What must have hit The Clash particularly hard was to see the right-wing, Washington-funded Contras adopt the group's favorite stance: that of the Rebels.

BROADWAY

Side 4's political content ends with the jazzy tones of 'Broadway', Strummer offering a life story from the perspective of a Manhattan street bum. But the lyric lacks focus, and the melody a chorus. This is less surprising when one discovers that 'Broadway' was among those *Sandinista!* songs "being written as they're going down (on tape)" as Strummer later described it.

The fourth side actually ends, somewhat inexplicably, with Mickey Gallagher's pre-pubescent children singing 'The Guns Of Brixton' to their dad's piano accompaniment before one of them finally satisfies listeners by instead announcing, "I'm tired of singing."

LOSE THIS SKIN

(Tymon Dogg)
By the time you've committed to a triple album, you're already in the realms of madness, so why not start your fifth side with a previously released recording credited to another artist? Tymon Dogg's 'Lose This Skin' had been recorded with Strummer, Jones, Headon, Gallagher and Watt-Roy as backing band at Electric Ladyland in New York, and then released as a single on Dogg's own label during the summer. Its re-appearance on *Sandinista!* suggests either an eventual scarcity of tracks to fill the self-determined quota, or a determination to promote Dogg on the back of the group's own significant clout.

'Lose This Skin' stands out as a significant musical diversion even for *Sandinista!*, but its violin-led ramshackle folk arrangement, and Dogg's gypsy whine, have a distinct charm, and it's a better song than many that follow. Dogg, who had known Strummer as a house-mate and busking partner since 1971, would eventually join Joe's post-Clash group The Mescaleros.

CHARLIE DON'T SURF

Another mid-tempo song, set to a softly syncopated soul rhythm, with Strummer and Jones singing lead in unison and Gallagher's organ riding high in the background. The title reference was obvious to anyone who had seen Francis Ford Coppola's 1979 Vietnam epic *Apocalypse Now* and witnessed Robert Duvall's memorable exclamation, as Lt. Col. Bill Kilgore setting off to surf, "I love the smell of napalm in the morning." The subject matter expands, as it did on 'Washington Bullets', to all "superpowers", perhaps to avoid accusations of lazy anti-Americanism. At almost five minutes, 'Charlie Don't Surf' is

yet *another* promising *Sandinista!* song that could have benefited from editing.

MENSFORTH HILL

The decision to take an earlier *Sandinista!* song – 'Something About England', as soon becomes apparent – and play it backwards, adding sound effects and non-sensical spoken word, could be seen as a noble avant-garde experiment, perhaps even a venture into the concept of *musique concrete*. But as reviewers were all too quick to point out, the idea owed itself, theoretically and musically, to The Beatles' 'Revolution No. 9', from that group's own sprawling *White Album*. As such, and unless it was intended as a wry tribute to the once Fab Four's own over-reaching, it's hard to justify its inclusion.

JUNKIE SLIP

Recorded in the same manner as 'Broadway' – "as it was being written" – with the lyrics committed to posterity before they could form a chorus. At least, unlike 'Broadway', the folksy arrangement lends itself to the loose structure, and for once, the experiment is kept under three minutes. It's easy to imagine Strummer's lyrics aimed in the direction of Headon's heroin addiction: the drummer's decline is clearly dragging the album down with it. But rock groups are notoriously protective about internal problems, and The Clash refused to publicly discuss Headon's increasing drug problems even as *Sandinista!* featured two songs about junkies.

KINGSTON ADVICE

The aborted visit to Kingston inspired this rock-reggae hybrid, with a resounding chorus and some interesting use of dub effects - especially on Strummer's vocals, as he suggests that the perennially violent edge of the Kingston ghettoes is at least partly due to "slavery under government". Not for the first time on *Sandinista!*, the listener is left certain that had the song been allowed to develop over time, 'Kingston Advice' could have become a confirmed Clash classic.

THE STREET PARADE

More unfinished - or incomplete - business. 'The Street Parade' has some bright sax playing (courtesy of Headon's old friend Gary Barnacle), steel drums mixed in a dub style, and polished vocals by both Strummer and Jones, indirect in their subject matter for once. In isolation – the notion of *Sandinista!* having so many great B-sides again returns as a back-handed compliment – 'The Street Parade' is intriguing. Coming at the end of five sides of often similarly rough-edged mixes, it's frustrating.

VERSION CITY

Fears that a sixth side of vinyl might be one too many were hardly eased by a thirty second introduction featuring an annoying (and irrelevant) upper crust voice, as if mimicking some sort of radio show. At least 'Version City' is close to a complete Clash song – more than can be said for anything that follows. Boarding the enduring myth of the musical train journey, and giving the folk-blues arrangement a slight dub mix (hence the reggae-friendly word 'Version' in the title), 'Version City' honours music's ability to transport listeners to previously unimagined destinations.

LIVING IN FAME

(Mikey Dread)

The version excursion continues with a heavy dub reggae track sung entirely by Mikey Dread. Aiming pointed barbs at The Selecter, The Specials and Madness for failing to "live up to your name", the words might seem vindictive toward a 2Tone movement that was keenly influenced by The Clash's own reggae crossovers – unless taken in the humour with which they were surely intended. 'Living In Fame' would have fitted in on Dread's own album *World War III* (recorded at Wessex around the same time, with Simonon playing bass on several cuts); its inclusion on *Sandinista!* therefore seems to satisfy the same purpose as Tymon Dogg's 'Lose This Skin', a generosity of spirit by a Clash eager to share their high profile with their musical travelers.

SILICONE ON SAPPHIRE

As the distinctive marimba steel drum rhythms of 'Washington Bullets' return, it's evident that 'Version City' is Side 6's one and only musical destination. (First time listeners, with the lyric sheet in front of them, would have noted the lack of words for any songs on Side 6 after the opening track.) As already stated, 'Washington Bullets' was one of *Sandinista!*'s more inspired performances, but with Strummer intoning unintelligibly over the backing track, and little of real dub imagination taking place in the rhythm, the exercise is wasted.

VERSION PARDNER

(Robert Ellen)

A more decidedly dub interpretation of Side 1's 'Junco Partner'. Stripped to its quietly pulsating rhythm track, augmented by Dread's box of aural tricks, stretched to almost five and a half minutes, it would pass as thoroughly Jamaican (or at least as authentically dread) to anyone who didn't recognise Strummer's occasionally interjected voice. The songwriting credit nonetheless goes to Robert Ellen again. (At time of *Sandinista!*'s original release, authorship of 'Junco Pardner' was unknown, and credited as such.)

CAREER OPPORTUNITIES

Desperation? Or inspiration? The decision to allow Mickey Gallagher's children Luke, Ben and Marcia to sing The Clash's 1977 anthem, backed by their dad's cheerful new chiming keyboard arrangement and a bare bones semi-acoustic Clash rhythm backing, has all the initial appeal of a school kids' talent show and about just as much longevity. It was a final nail in the coffin for many, *many* Clash fans. But the singalong serves two extra-curricular purposes. Firstly, it demonstrates that 'Career Opportunities', stripped of electric guitars and dole-queue chants, was at heart a great pop song. Secondly, subtly, it reminded listeners that unemployment in Britain had continued to rise drastically since the song was written in 1976, and that schoolchildren had every reason to fear for their own working futures. Still, it's hard to believe that the Gallagher kids, whose voices had yet to break, understood any of this, and the second verse is duly reworded to address petty school rules instead.

SHEPHERDS DELIGHT
(Dread/Clash)
For even the most ardent Clash fan, *Sandinista!* could now not end soon enough, to which purpose the instrumental 'Shepherds Delight' takes its sweet time. A semi-acoustic dub recording made with Mikey Dread in Manchester at the same time as 'Bankrobber', it had already been revamped and used as backing for 'If Music Could Talk', and the melody, as such, was perilously close to 'Living In Fame'... But by this point in proceedings, who was seriously keeping track? Two minutes of laid-back rhythm and the album ends with an equally half-hearted, if persistent, explosion. After almost two and a half hours, *Sandinista!* is over.

THIS IS RADIO CLASH 7"/12"
(November 1981)
The poor state of British radio had long been a source of inspiration for The Clash. They had sung about it on the vituperative 'Capital Radio', and as recently as the 'Hitsville U.K.' B-side, had allowed Mikey Dread to wax lyrical about the poor state of 'Radio 1'. Along the way, The Clash had frequently expressed a desire to launch their own radio station, and in early 1981, after Joe Strummer re-hired Bernie Rhodes as manager, they revived the idea. In the absence of actual access to the airwaves, they recorded 'This Is Radio Clash' as the first in a projected series of recorded radio broadcasts. Typically for The Clash, it was also the last.

Musically, 'This Is Radio Clash' is inspired by the music of New York, where a wide range of FM radio stations offered an abundance of listening choice unimaginable to stifled British kids. Paul Simonon's relatively rigid bass line and the fact that the song was recorded in London – with Gary Barnacle on saxophone – may explain why it nonetheless has a more firmly pronounced rock feel than either 'The Magnificent Seven' or 'Lightning Strikes'.

Perhaps because the song stemmed from a propagandist platform, as opposed to Strummer's increasingly poetic way of looking at the world's problems, 'This Is Radio Clash' proved short on lyrical substance. But the various remixes ('Radio Clash', 'Radio 5', 'Radio 6', 'Outside Broadcast' and 'Radio Five 4' scattered among various British and American 7" and 12" releases) allowed Mick Jones to bring his New York obsession to the fore, employing all manner of contemporary studio techniques and declaring his own intended musical direction.

COMBAT ROCK

(Album, May 1982)

The final album by the classic Clash line-up also proved to be the group's most popular, for which there are several explanations. *Combat Rock* contained the group's two biggest hits ('Should I Stay Or Should I Go' and 'Rock The Casbah'); it was a single serving of just twelve songs; it was mixed to conventional aural standards by veteran producer Glyn Johns; the group toured heavily before, during and after its release, securing crucial record company support; they made a suitably silly video that was a shoo-in with the newly influential MTV; they played stadiums as opening act for The Who; and, as much as anything, public awareness of The Clash had been growing around the world for the last five years, needing only the right record to send the band into superstar stratosphere. *Combat Rock* was that record. Being The Clash, the group celebrated their overdue success by breaking apart at the seams.

Bad blood was in fact festering throughout the recording process. Joe Strummer wanted to revisit his original plan for *London Calling* – recording straight to tape - and The Rolling Stones' mobile studio was duly attached to the group's rehearsal studios, Ear, right by the Westway. But after an interim tour, Mick Jones insisted they return to familiar surroundings: Electric Ladyland in New York. Months later, by which time engineer Jerry Green had been brought over from London in

a failed attempt to rein in the affair, Jones presented the rest of the band with a fifteen-song double album. They rejected it.

Never ones to do things in the right order, The Clash had booked their first tour of the Far East and Australasia for early 1982, expecting to promote the new album. Instead, they found themselves in a Sydney studio during a 'Magnificent Seven' run of shows in the Australian capital, trying to mix something palatable to all four members. Given their state of hearing (let along state of mind) following the two hour nightly concerts, the process was a disaster and contributed to Strummer collapsing from exhaustion on stage a week later. Pennie Smith came on tour in Thailand to photograph an album cover and captured the group looking not straight into the camera as had always been their nature, but shirking it, as if unwilling to acknowledge their fractured status. Back in Britain, Glyn Johns – with Strummer alongside him, not Jones - speedily rescued the recordings, performing the kind of clinical editing and mixing operation that many would love to have heard on *Sandinista!* After months of doubt, *Combat Rock* suddenly sounded like a hit album, and was lined up for a mid-May release.

Then, in late April, on the eve of a lengthy UK tour, Joe Strummer went missing. When he returned, after almost a month, Topper Headon promptly left the band. Terry Chimes – drummer on The Clash's debut album – was hastily re-recruited for an American tour starting the following week. *Combat Rock* was released into this confused Clash landscape, and promptly raced up global charts on its way to selling several million copies.

Strummer's disappearance had been instigated at Rhodes' behest as a way to cancel the UK tour's slow-selling opening Scottish dates. After initially going along with the idea, Strummer regretted letting the fans down and called Rhodes' bluff by disappearing for real, surviving incognito in France for several weeks until Kosmo Vinyl tracked him down. He used the time to think through the group's future: Strummer knew *Combat Rock* could reap long overdue rewards, and he saw that opportunity potentially wasted on power struggles and the dead weight of a junkie drummer. By causing the postponement of a UK tour, Strummer confirmed that *he* was irreplaceable, and by returning to demand the ousting of the group's now unreliable drummer, gave notice that no one else was safe in The Clash, not even Mick Jones.

In retrospect, it was life imitating art. Strummer had absorbed the new Clash album's theme of "post combat stress disorder", willingly provoking his own cinematic showdown a la Travis Bickle in the 1976 Martin Scorcese movie *Taxi Driver*. It was no coincidence that Strummer was soon sporting a Mohawk as per Bickle, nor that he had become close friends with the character's actor, Robert de Niro. In fact *Combat Rock* (working title *Rat Patrol From Fort Bragg*), was the musical counterpart to *Taxi Driver*, taking the concept of urban America – specifically, New York – in the wake of the Vietnam War and then running rampant with it. Such a firm American focus did not detract, this time round, from British sales.

Combat Rock is not a classic album. It lacks the violent revolt of *The Clash and* the guitar grandeur of *Give 'Em Enough Rope*. It comes not close to *London Calling*'s combination of enthusiasm, energy and experimentation. It almost abandons the group's long-standing association with reggae. But it's a memorable swan song because, apart from two of the group's finest slow songs ('Ghetto Defendant' and 'Straight To Hell') and some solid album tracks, it was home to a couple of anthems that couldn't be contained by the album itself, bursting out of the LP grooves to become global hits, establishing their permanent presence in the pop music landscape. And so The Clash journey was completed.

KNOW YOUR RIGHTS

Clash fans longing for a return to the old ways were no doubt encouraged by Strummer's initial assurance,

"This is a public service announcement – with *guitar*." But what threatens to be a raucous manifesto turns out to be a series of limited lyrical gestures set to a primarily one-chord jam. A rockabilly rhythm keeps the beat flowing but it's hard to hear 'Know Your Rights' as a complete song. That might explain why its release as a British single failed to light up the charts.

CAR JAMMING

By its title and its references to ghetto blasters in the shape of "King Kong cassettes", 'Car Jamming' is clearly influenced by urban America. A Bo Diddley-like beat leaves plenty room for Jones to offer funky guitar stabs, as his girlfriend Ellen Foley joins in on backing vocals. Joe Strummer, meanwhile, furthers the album's theme with a line about Vietnam vets hustling for change "riding Aluminum crutches", as was sadly a common sight in American cities at the time. As with its predecessor, 'Car Jamming' sounds like something less than a full song, though Glyn Johns' mix ensures that it holds attention.

SHOULD I STAY OR SHOULD I GO

Combat Rock's two hit singles are layered with ironies such as make the rock'n'roll world go round. At time of recording, Mick Jones was so fully immersed in New York hip-hop that he had earned himself the not entirely complementary nickname Wack Attack. Yet at that same time, he wrote, recorded and sung his most well-known Clash song as a straight-up radio-friendly rock'n'roll anthem. Built around a classic power chord riff, its sing-along qualities greatly emphasised by a sparse but emphatically loud mix, 'Should I Stay Or Should I Go' finds Jones mustering his strongest singing voice to date, pondering his romantic dilemma, and concluding that he can't win. Joe Ely, visiting Electric Ladyland at the time, was recruited to sing backing vocals with Strummer – which they switched to Spanish. (Tape engineer Eddie Garcia secured the translation over the phone from his mother. To subsequent accusations that the wording was wrong, Strummer would bluff that they had been singing in "Ecuadorean Spanish".) It was an inspired move, lending an otherwise simple song a necessary dose of mystery.

As a single, 'Should I Stay Or Should I Go' – remixed by Mick Jones with Bob Clearmountain as Engineer - fared better in both British and American charts than anything since the *London Calling* period; a decade later it became a British number one hit after being used in a Levi's television commercial.

ROCK THE CASBAH

Topper Headon had been carrying a self-composed piano riff around for years. At Electric Ladyland one day, before the other band members arrived, he laid down that piano part, with a crisp drum track and flowing bass line behind it. When the others showed up, they were immediately impressed and demanded to work with this 'demo'. To protestations that it was only two minutes long, they merely spliced it and doubled it to form a full song. It was rare for The Clash to find Topper so productive, and equally rare to be forced to work with a short backing track: Bernie Rhodes had complained during the London sessions that everything was as long as "a raga". Strummer now used that comment as a springboard for a lyric inspired primarily by the newly fundamentalist Iran, where people were being whipped for owning disco records. (As a boy, Joe had spent time in Iran with his diplomat parents.) His intelligent but witty lyric quickly established dancing as a natural human instinct, and imagined a Bedouin groove so intense that the King's jet fighter pilots refused to put it down.

It's a strong assertion of belief in the universal power of music, given further credence – and humour - in a video clip depicting a Sheik and an Orthodox Jew dancing (and drinking) round a swimming pool together as The Clash look on in bemusement. One person is missing from the scene: Nicky Headon, sacked just as the album was released. 'Rock The Casbah' stands as testament to the drummer's all-round musical talents (the piano playing is as nimble as anything Mickey Gallagher ever contributed), but also to their waste. As all songs on *Combat Rock* were again credited to The Clash as a unit, Headon received no special compensation for 'Rock The Casbah', but his share in all the other songs ensured he could continue to finance his heroin addiction for years to come.

Glyn Johns' album mix sounds like it's already imagining itself on the radio: the vocals are up front, there are hand-claps in all the right places, backing chants just where you need them, percussive and toy keyboard overdubs in the third verse, and guitars that come in only occasionally but highly effectively. But as per 'Should I Stay Or Should I Go', Mick Jones re-mixed the song for its single release. 'Rock The Casbah' peaked in America at number eight late in 1982, after several months' strong publicity and their stadium shows with The Who. It was their only US Top 10 single.

RED ANGEL DRAGNET

A Paul Simonon melody and vocal, though with less of a reggae emphasis than in the past. The bassist mostly chants his way through a Strummer-improved lyric inspired by the shooting death of Guardian Angel Frank Melvin, on December 30 1981, while the Clash were in New York, recording. The volunteer vigilantes Guardian Angels were a controversial development in New York – a sign that the city could no longer police itself – but they had become a reasonably common sight. In Newark, New Jersey, just across the Hudson, their presence was less familiar, and local Chapter leader Melvin was shot dead by a local police patrol who misidentified him as an aggressor. The Clash seize on the front page news to heavy-handedly indulge their *Taxi Driver* obsession, with Kosmo Vinyl impersonating Robert De Niro's Travis Bickle, repeating one of the movie's more memorable monologues. Unlike other songs on *Combat Rock*, at least 'Red Angel

THE CLASH
MUSIC THAT MATTERS

1952

August 21
John Mellor, the future Joe Strummer, born in Ankara, Turkey. The son of a diplomat, he attends boarding school in England.

1955

June 26
Mick Jones born in Clapham, South London.

1955

May 30
Nicky Headon born in Bromley, Kent.

1955

December 15
Paul Simonon born in Brixton, South London.

THE CLASH
MUSIC THAT MATTERS

1974

Mellor renames himself Joe Strummer ("because I can only play all six string at once, or none at all"), and returns to London from Newport Art School in Wales. Out of a squat in Maida Vale, he forms the 101'ers, who quickly make a name on London's thriving "pub rock" circuit.

1976

July 4
With Keith Levene as second guitarist and Terry Chimes on drums, The Clash play their debut gig, opening for the Sex Pistols in Sheffield.

1975

August
Jones and James meet Bernie Rhodes at the Nashville in Kensington. Rhodes, who has been involved in setting up the Sex Pistols, offers to manage them.

1976

September 20
The Clash play as part of the London Punk Festival at the 100 Club, alongside the Sex Pistols, Subway Sect and Siouxsie and the Banshees. Levene having departed, it is their first gig as a four-piece.

December
In disagreements over the group's overt political stance, Terry Chimes quits on the eve of the 'Anarchy In The UK Tour,' which sees the Clash bottom of the bill to the Sex Pistols, the Damned and Johnny Thunders' Heartbreakers. Rob Harper takes Chimes' place, but most shows are canceled as a result of anti-Pistols/punk rock hysteria.

January 1
The Clash appear on the cover of *Sounds* as the music paper's "pick for '77."

THE CLASH

THE ICA, that home of lively experiment in London's fall, is fast becoming the badly needed workshop-cum-watering hole for the growing number of nightly ravers following the rise and rise of the new-wave punk-rock bands.

Last Saturday, advertised as a Night Of Pure Energy, was the second in a projected series. In a spartan environment (a large, square room with an excellent view of the stage) a warm crush of people gathered to parade their finery and check out the band most likely (now that the Sex Pistols are signed-up and on their way) to become the "enfants terribles" of the scene.

The Clash are big news now. As soon as they set foot on stage they slam into their set. Terry Chimes (drums) cracks out the tempo, Mick Jones (guitar) and Paul Simenon (bass) hit on their low-slung guitars, and Joe Strummer, wrenching a list at his side, tangles his gaping mouth at the mike. They're off — and, like the expert emotional marksmen they are, never do they embellish a single action with anything more than what is absolutely necessary to get to the heart of the matter as effectively as possible.

"White Riot" is their first number. It's their theme song. Their "Anarchy In The UK", and it's a fine introduction to the electrifying pace to come. So fast do these musicians attack their set that it's impossible to imagine them noticing the place was collapsing around them. When the black shape of Patti Smith leaps on stage in front of Paul Simenon it hardly falters.

But perhaps the band do register that one of their favourite rock outfits is now in the audience, too (they all went to see Patti the night before) because, from that moment on, there's no stopping them. Even though Joe Strummer's guitar (which he has 'treated' so that it rings with an extraordinary treble sound) claps out before he can mash into the second number, "London's burning," they visibly pull out all the stops and deliver the most concise set they've yet played in public. — CAROLINE COON.

November
The Clash are the subject of a major profile in *Melody Maker* by Caroline Coon.

January-February
With live sound engineer Mickey Foote as producer and Terry Chimes – credited as Tory Crimes – agreeing to record the songs as a favour to the group, The Clash record their first album in fifteen days.

1978

June-July
The 'Out On Parole' tour travels
through the UK.

1979

February
A brief tour of the States in support of
Give 'Em Enough Rope, the band's first
official American release.

1979

May-June
Moving into Vanilla
Studios in Pimlico, the
Clash undertake daily
rehearsals, formulating
the songs that will
become *London Calling*

1980

January
London Calling is released in the United
States. It makes the Top 30 there in March.

1979

July
. re-packaged edition
debut LP *The Clash*,
ncluding many of the
subsequent non-LP
single tracks, is
released in America,
th 'I Fought The Law'
elected as the band's
first Stateside single.

1981

September
Eight nights at the
Theatre Mogador in Paris.

1980

May-June
The 'Sixteen Tons' tour
resumes through Europe
and the UK.

1981

October
The 'Radio Clash' tour of the
UK concludes with seven nights
at the Lyceum in London.

1982

May
Strummer returns from hiding on
the eve of *Combat Rock*'s release
and insists that Headon is fired for
his heroin addiction. Terry Chimes
returns as drummer for the
imminent American tour.

1981

November
'This Is Radio Clash,' a natural
musical follow-on from 'The
Magnificent Seven', released as a
single in various formats and mixes.

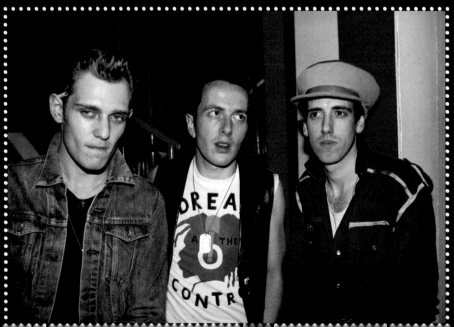

1982

May-June
The 'Casbah Club'
tour of America
includes five nights
at the Hollywood
Palladium in
Los Angeles

1983

1983

October
Strummer and Simonon,
with Pete Howard staying
on drums, advertise for
new members of the
Clash. Guitarists Nick
Sheppard and Vince
White pass the audition.

1983

August
Rehearsals for a new album grind to a halt in disputes over
musical direction. Jones refuses to sign new management
contract with Rhodes.

January
The new-look, back-to-basics
Clash plays six dates in California.

1985

June-August
The Clash play sporadic European
festivals. The Greek Music Festival in
Athens on 27 August, in front of 40,000, is
their last. Strummer disappears immediately
afterwards to Spain for a month.

1985

September
A single, 'This Is England',
is released alongside the
LP *Cut The Crap*. The
single is well-received; the
album is panned.
Strummer returns after
the negative reaction to
announce the permanent
break-up of the band
called The Clash.

Dragnet' acknowledges its cinematic influence in other lyrics. Fashion note: The Guardian Angels' all-red clothing – with red beret on top – was adopted by Mick Jones during the following year's touring.

STRAIGHT TO HELL

One of the "ragas" of which Bernie Rhodes had complained, 'Straight To Hell' was edited down in London but still came in at five and a half minutes, the longest track on the album. Unlike many such songs on *Sandinista!*, the time passes quickly: 'Straight To Hell' is the emotional cornerstone of *Combat Rock*, its subtle, slow groove snaking under the listener's skin like a tropical virus. Headon suggested the syncopated bossa nova drum pattern and then enlisted Strummer to bang the bass drum with a lemonade bottle wrapped in a towel for emphasis. Strummer's words – mixed right up front - are the deepest on the album, starting in Britain, moving to Vietnam and ending up in "junkieland" USA. On closer inspection, they're at least partially telling the tale of kids born to American soldiers and their Vietnamese lovers during the lengthy war in South-East Asia, and the confused nationality issues that resulted. At one key point, Strummer tells "bamboo kid" his blood "ain't coca-cola, it's rice". It may just be coincidence, but on the back of the lyric sheet, designed this time by New York graffiti artist Futura 2000 (who had been touring with The Clash as a real-time backdrop designer), The Clash are depicted in Thailand drinking Coca-Cola.

OVERPOWERED BY FUNK

A self-evident slice of hard-hitting Clash funk, though lacking new ideas to better 'The Magnificent Seven' and 'This Is Radio Clash'. White funk had become the new sound of the hip London streets by 1981, attempted with varying degrees of authenticity by everyone from former punk peers The Jam (the intro to 'Overpowered By Funk' is the same as that group's single 'Absolute Beginners') to New Romantics Spandau Ballet and current teenyboppers Haircut 100. 'Overpowered By Funk' was

originally recorded in the British capital and Strummer ribs its trendiness: "Don't you love our western ways?" Once in New York, the group recruited Futura 2000 to deliver a powerful rap in a late-song role that would previously have been taken by reggae toaster Mikey Dread. This shift in Clash musical focus is acknowledged in the opening line: "If you ain't reggae for it... funk out."

ATOM TAN

The shortest song on *Combat Rock*, 'Atom Tan' gains relevance in hindsight, as anyone who has ever heard Mick Jones' post-Clash group Big Audio Dynamite will instantly understand. As a blueprint for Jones' future, 'Atom Tan' is sketchy, but the call-and-response double-tracked vocals, the pointed guitar riffs, and especially, the ascending and descending melodies, are all in place. The only thing missing is the hip-hop groove: Headon fills in with modest "machine gun" rolls.

SEAN FLYNN

Named for Errol Flynn's son, a journalist who went missing in Cambodia in 1970, at the height of the war in neighbouring Vietnam, and recorded at the same time as 'This Is Radio Clash'. Gary Barnacle again plays saxophone, extemporising with considerable imagination across a track that is deliberately cinematic, lacking a clear beat or melody and succeeding less obviously on album than it might have done as part of a real soundtrack. Strummer's lyrics are unusually succinct, however; they envisage Flynn heading off to his destiny with death while allowing the music to do most of the talking.

GHETTO DEFENDANT

Combat Rock's lone diversion into proper reggae, though the sound of revered beat poet Allen Ginsberg on the microphone indicates how far the group have moved on from their dub infatuation. Ginsberg had made acquaintance with The Clash after joining them on stage during their lengthy residency at Times Square casino Bond's in June 1981, and stopped in at

Electric Ladyland hoping to recruit the group to his own album. They instead recruited him to theirs, which was a smart move: Ginsberg brings to 'Ghetto Defendant' a quietly authoritative secondary voice that traverses the world's war-torn hot spots past and present as Strummer, in his best Kingston warrior style, sings with palpable emotion of inner-city junkies. (By now, it's obvious that Strummer could not, in good conscience, promote *Combat Rock* with a heroin addict in the band.) As with 'Straight To Hell', with which 'Ghetto Defendant' forms something of a pair, the slow pace allows the song to breathe and expand until it becomes essential listening, suggesting that The Clash had, at the final hurdle, learned the all-important difference between "album track" and "unfinished, unmixed jam". All the same, a final verse was lopped off at mixing stage to fit everything on vinyl.

INOCULATED CITY

Even more so than 'Atom Tan', 'Inoculated City' could easily have appeared on a post-Clash Big Audio Dynamite album - especially as, this time out, Jones sings all vocals, the drum rhythm is crisp and driving, and there's an American TV commercial included as indication of his growing infatuation with samples. In the absence of Strummer's usual vocal presence, Jones' singing voice is at its strongest, and he triple-tracks it across the stereo spectrum, a trick he would frequently repeat with B.A.D. The anti-war lyrics proved particularly poignant when Britain went to war with Argentina over the Falkland Islands just before the album's release. It's interesting that Jones was usually the one accused of stretching Clash albums out beyond all common sense of length, yet his B.A.D. blueprints are *Combat Rock*'s two shortest songs.

DEATH IS A STAR

Combat Rock concludes in quietly jazzy style, melancholy piano accompanied by synthesised strings and brushed drums. But The Clash never did do schmaltz and the lyrics offer instead one last

journey into the jungle's heart of darkness. Appropriately, given that the hand-off between Strummer's spoken words and Mick Jones' sung vocals form something of a duet, and that the arrangement is similar to that of a show tune farewell, it would be the last time Strummer and Jones were heard on record together as The Clash.

CUT THE CRAP

(September 1985)

The Clash existed long before Nicky Headon joined – they recorded *The Clash* album without him - and so it seemed fair to assume they could continue after the drummer was fired. But The Clash had never existed without Mick Jones; he was the founding member and the original driving force, besides which, the group dynamic had always fed off the songwriting and vocal talents of the Strummer-Jones partnership. Contradictory though they may have been as personalities, the pair served to complement each other as musicians: just as Joe Strummer carefully sabotaged many of Mick Jones' most conventional recordings, ensuring the guitarist did not turn the band into rock'n'roll clichés, so Jones, with his inspired arrangements and considerable studio skills, served to prevent Strummer's often confused polemics from ending up like so much soap-box oratory. For the punk generation, the Strummer-Jones partnership carried no less import than that of Lennon-McCartney or Jagger-Richards, and it was equally impossible to envisage a Clash without the pair of them than it was to imagine The Beatles or The Rolling Stones without their *own* dual leadership.

The right thing for Joe Strummer to do, if he was so unhappy with Mick Jones that he could no longer bear to be in a band with him, was to break up The Clash. But in the heat of battle for complete control, he preferred to be rid his long-term partner and claim The Clash as his own. He was encouraged in this regard by manager Bernie Rhodes, who then insisted The Clash continue, or rather revert, to a 1977 punk rock group. With Paul Simonon faithfully in tow (the bassist, whose loyalty should by rights have been with his longer-standing musical partner, had also had enough of Jones' arrogance and petulance), Strummer and Rhodes hired three new band members: Nick Sheppard and Vince White on guitars, and Pete Howard on drums. The new-look Clash toured America and Britain in early 1984, drawing good crowds, and a certain amount of support in Britain for airing new songs that addressed the increasingly polarised society under Prime Minister Thatcher. But this encouragement was offset by the clear understanding that the group was journeying backwards musically.

The final Clash album, if it can be called that, was something less than a team effort. Having worked up the new songs, Strummer and Rhodes – the manager now taking on Mick Jones' role as the front man's musical partner – went to Munich in December 1984 and recorded backing tracks, not with the new musicians, but with hired German engineers programming the drum and keyboard parts. The three new band members, and Simonon, were then brought over to provide overdubs – and backing vocals – early the following year. White and Sheppard ended up playing guitar on most songs; Howard is not heard playing on the album; rumour has it that Norman Watts-Roy again played bass.

If it seems unlike Strummer to let his usually close attention to detail wander, it's partly

understandable: he lost both his parents and became a father himself within the space of a few months around this time. Again, in retrospect, the right thing to do would have been to take an extended leave of absence, but by now he was again in the financial hole, as Jones put a freeze on Clash assets. Rhodes took full advantage of Strummer's confused state, claiming co-songwriting authorship on the new material. (Simonon, who at least had a share in *Sandinista!* and *Combat Rock*, was left out entirely.) By the time Strummer came to realise that the new Clash, especially the new Clash album, was but a poor man's caricature of 1977 Clash, it was too late: Rhodes had finished mixing what was now to be called *Cut The Crap* (crediting the job to Jose Unidos), and CBS was anxious to release it to what they thought would prove a hungry public.

Contractually, Strummer had put himself in a situation he couldn't control, and emotionally, he wasn't up to the fight anyway. Still, he pulled off one last pure punk move – taking the five-piece around the UK on an unadvertised, unorchestrated busking tour, hitch-hiking from town to town where they would play outside concert venues, in the town square or alongside the local church - before disappearing from sight on the eve of *Cut The Crap*'s release. He returned just in time for the predictably withering reviews – and to announce to the rest of the group that The Clash were no more. Over subsequent years, he was almost able to convince the fans that *Cut The Crap* was never released; unfortunately it remains on sale, an offensive blemish on The Clash's otherwise remarkable output.

 THE DICTATOR
As if deliberately ensuring that *Cut The Crap* should immediately alienate as many Clash fans as possible, 'The Dictator' opens proceedings with poorly programmed drums, cheap synths, and inaudible vocals set to an imitation of a melody, all drowned out by rival conversations as if recorded over several crossed telephone

lines, while the backing boys shout and chant seemingly at random. Lyrics on the album sleeve – the cover to which was itself an embarrassing cartoon of punk clichés – suggest that the maturity of 'Spanish Bombs' and 'Washington Bullets' had fallen by the wayside for cheap polemics.

DIRTY PUNK

Grungy guitar riffs initially suggest something approaching a proper Clash anthem, but the wafer-thin programmed drums and Strummer's buried vocals cancel out such optimism all too quickly. Likewise, there's something of a real chorus on offer here, though as becomes a regular occurrence on *Cut The Crap*, it's quickly rendered hollow by the boot boy vocals.

WE ARE THE CLASH

Musically, one of *Cut The Crap*'s more promising offerings. Strummer is singing something like a tune (making first known reference to the Nineties genre Britpop), and the guitar riffs, while they owe more of a debt to Steve Jones of the Pistols than Mick Jones, have a certain simplistic charm. The programmed beats still sound like exactly what they are – rhythms recorded on the cheap by jobbing Germans – but they're not the worst on the album. Yet these positives are quickly canceled out by the song's overall conceit. "We are The Clash" sing the terraced throngs of new group members, as if this excuses anything and everything. "No, you're not," the listeners scream back from their bedrooms, astounded at the horror of it all: you're a pale imitation of Sham 69 at the disco.

ARE YOU RED..Y?

An inner sleeve communiqué to *Cut The Crap*, dated October '85, offered a tired Bernie Rhodes call to arms. But even the manager, and supposed co-songwriter, balked at calling a song 'Are You Ready For War?' and shortened it for the album, though in doing so he changed the title's connotation to socialist/communist red. One of the new guitarists plays a riff not out of line with B.A.D.'s spaghetti western

infatuations, and though the synth parts are pure mid-Eighties cheese, there's something of a song building here. Yet again, it's let down by inaudible vocals, terrace chants and lack of forward movement.

COOL UNDER HEAT

Leaving the anticipated shouted chorus aside, 'Cool Under Heat' actually works. There's a simple, fuzzed up guitar riff such as Mick Jones would eat for breakfast, the welcome sound of an acoustic guitar and the surprise of an audible opening lyric, even if it is just the tired cliché of "Rebels on the corner". It's apparent now that some of these songs could have worked well if presented by a truly new band – something not called The Clash – and if, instead of the cheap programming and muffled mix, they had been performed as a unit under the auspices of a professional producer. But they weren't.

MOVERS AND SHAKERS

Unfortunately, the opening line is also discernible on this song, and it's excruciating: "The boy stood in the burning slum". Worse still, the entire lyric is on the album sleeve, and it comes across as a Thatcherite reversal of 'Career Opportunities'. Whereas The Clash of 1977 demanded, crucially, the right *not* to work, The Clash of 1985 suggests that it's okay for a man "to accept what he gets thrown… 'cos times are bad and he's making good." This would be patronising stuff even from a fellow dole queue veteran, but coming from the lips of a successful (if contradictory) rock star, it borders on the offensive. Fortunately for Strummer, not enough people were listening to be truly offended – or he might have been first up against the wall come his beloved revolution.

THIS IS ENGLAND

There are several reasons 'This Is England', which opened vinyl Side 2, succeeds while everything around it fails. It's noticeably slower - and therefore more sparse - than the other songs. There's the interesting use of samples, some proper harmonies, acoustic guitars, and a blistering electric guitar riff that's made more powerful by virtue of breathing space. The tempo allows Strummer to sing, as opposed to shout, and his voice carries some hint of melancholy and nostalgia, as opposed to the usual trite melodrama. His vision of England 1984 – the year he wrote the song, and the year of George Orwell's famed novel of a fascist society – is at once sad and vehement. And though references to the Falklands War of the "South Atlantic" were outdated by late 1985, the line "This is England, that I'm supposed to die for" is all the more effective for its rhetorical nature.

There was no shortage of conscientious objectors to Thatcherite England, and some of them were doing very well in the charts: The Smiths, The Housemartins, The Style Council (featuring former Jam front man Paul Weller) and Billy Bragg had all found ways to cover controversial subject matter in a commercial manner, and had even come together as a collective under the cleverly-named (if ultimately disorganised) Red Wedge. 'This Is England' is the one song from *Cut The Crap* that merits favorable comparison to the Clash's mid-Eighties competition and, released as a single in advance of the album, it even made the British top 30.

Yet the most curious aspect of 'This Is England' is how much, in retrospect, it has come to sound like for Big Audio Dynamite. Take away the chorus chant, imagine Mick Jones on vocals, and it would easily fit on any number of B.A.D. albums. This makes it even harder to understand why, if Mick Jones was exiled partly for having moved into a different musical universe, he and Strummer found themselves at such a similar creative point only a year or so later. Then again, Jones made a new career out of this sound; Strummer used it only as a brief departure from an otherwise awful album.

THREE CARD TRICK

An unexpected but welcome use of the ska beat. (Unfortunately, the four-to-the-floor electronic drum beat rather offsets

the intent.) And the lyrics, the last of three to be printed on the album sleeve, rise above the facile, though Strummer's belief in the working class – as ready, willing and able to take on the forces of power - appears to have moved beyond pure optimism into blind belief.

PLAY TO WIN

The Space Invaders soundtrack is reminiscent of *Sandinista!*'s 'Ivan Meets G.I. Joe', and the lyric has a familiar sense of international competition. But it's let down by inaudible backchat and a chant about the "wild frontier" that seems too close to former punk Adam Ant's glam pop persona for comfort.

FINGERPOPPIN'

One of the only songs on *Cut The Crap* to avoid the terrace chorus and the political rhetoric and, unsurprisingly, one of the few that shows long-term potential. Set to a funky Eighties keyboard brass riff, Strummer's lyric is an uplifting throwback to The Clash of *Sandinista!* and, with some quality production, the song could just about have made that triple album's frequently low quality bar.

NORTH AND SOUTH

Back to divided Thatcherite Britain, and though Strummer eschews solo lead for the equally coarse double-tracked vocals of his fellow band members, at least that excuses them from showing up to shout their way through another chorus. The melody is strong, but the production is simply too busy to make sense of what might once have become a decent ballad.

LIFE IS WILD

The vague promise of *Cut The Crap*'s second half is fully extinguished by a return to its initial clumsiness. In particular, there's a similar invasion of outside noises that made 'The Dictator' almost unlistenable. Somewhere in the midst of this, Strummer – and cohorts – are urgently trying to insist that everyone's having a good time. The claim rings painfully hollow.

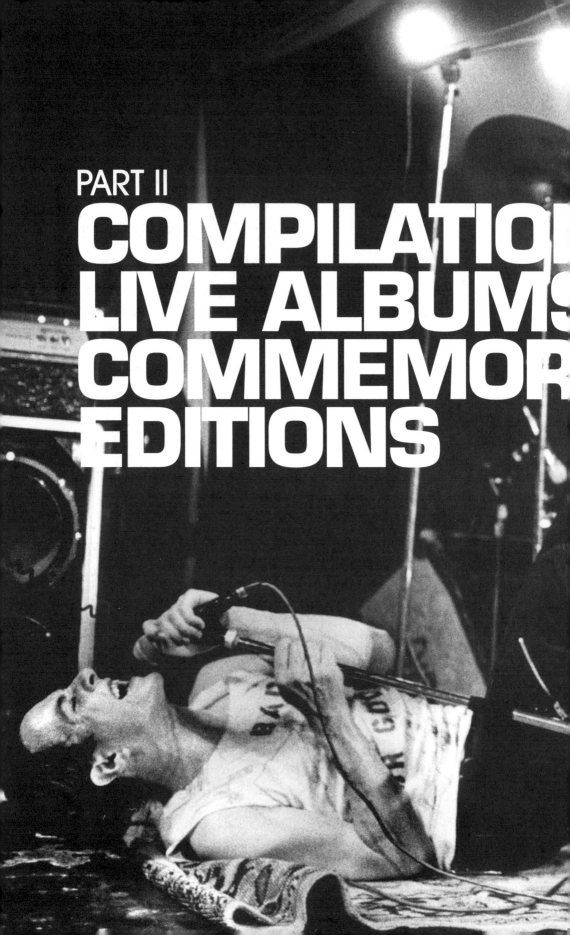

PART II
COMPILATION
LIVE ALBUMS
COMMEMOR
EDITIONS

THE STORY OF THE CLASH
Volume 1

(UK, April 1998)

Disc 1: The Magnificent Seven/Rock The Casbah/This Is Radio Clash/Should I Stay Or Should I Go/Straight To Hell/Armagideon Time/Clampdown/Train In Vain/The Guns Of Brixton/I Fought The Law/Somebody Got Murdered/Lost In The Supermarket/ Bank Robber

Disc 2: (White Man) In Hammersmith Palais/London's Burning/Janie Jones/Tommy Gun/Complete Control/Capital Radio/White Riot/ Career Opportunities/City Rockers/Safe European Home/Stay Free/London Calling/ Spanish Bombs/English Civil War/Police & Thieves (March 1988)

The first 'Best Of' compilation, and the only one originally released on (double) vinyl, *The Story Of The Clash* collects pretty much all the right songs and then compiles them in all the wrong order - primarily so that the most commercial songs get up-front precedence. As such, *The Story Of The Clash* just about works its way backwards through the group's career, including its three *Combat Rock* cuts among the first five selections and saving all the 1977 recordings for the second album. The sleeve notes are written by Strummer as 'Albert Transom', an omnipresent fictional valet: they're a humourous insiders' memory of all the good times on tour, and evoke a better sense of the group's adventures than any number of typically straight-faced chronological liner notes.

Most of the songs are the single versions, several making what was then their debut appearances on CD. 'Clash City Rockers' is the faster mix. 'The Magnificent Seven' is a minute shorter than on *Sandinista!* 'Should I Stay Or Should I Go' and 'Rock The Casbah' are Mick Jones' re-mixed single versions, as engineered by Bob Clearmountain. The former is almost identical to the album version; the latter is murkier, with piano and guitars brought to the fore, more prominent use of sound effects, and the toy synth sound of the third verse lowered.

ARMAGIDEON TIME
(W. Williams/J. Mittoo)
First appearance on CD for the 'London Calling' B-side. The 1979 cult reggae hit by Willie Williams offered perfect subject matter for The Clash, and their studio rendition, a little funky with bright chimes over the top, came out as well as any reggae song on *London Calling*. The muffled voice at the three minute mark is Kosmo Vinyl letting Joe know that they were overstepping their intended recording time. The singer's response - "Okay okay, don't push us when we're hot!" – is delivered in perfect rhythm, and sounds like it was fully rehearsed. Such are the ways with great recordings.

CAPITAL RADIO
(Strummer-Jones)
Released as part of a 7" EP for *NME* readers who sent in a coupon from the April 2 1977 edition, in which The Clash were featured on the cover and interviewed inside by Tony Parsons. Included here (and only here) in its full 5:20 version, 'Capital Radio' starts with segments from that interview, recorded on the London Underground's Circle Line and of great historical interest if not exactly essential listening. The actual song 'Capital Radio' kicks in just after three minutes; with its punchy guitar riff, simplistic bass and half-shouted, half-harmonised vocals, it would have fitted in perfectly on *The Clash*. The comments about the lyrics (see *The Cost Of Living* EP), remain absolutely applicable: this was one of the bravest and most suicidal statements made by any 1977 punk band.

THE SINGLES

(UK, November 1991; USA, October 1999)

White Riot/Remote Control/Complete Control/Clash City Rockers/(White Man) In Hammersmith Palais/Tommy Gun/English Civil War/I Fought The Law/London Calling/Train In Vain/Bankrobber/The Call Up/Hitsville U.K./The Magnificent Seven/This Is Radio Clash/Know Your Rights/Rock The Casbah/Should I Stay Or Should I Go

A one-CD set compiling all the British singles in chronological order, released in the group's home country to capitalise on the chart-topping Levi's-sponsored success of 'Should I Stay Or Should I Go'. *The Singles* includes the sub-standard 'Remote Control' as second track, but as evidence that The Clash were still rewriting their history, does not include the post-Jones line-up's 'This Is England' at the end. These are strictly the versions released to the public back when the public still bought 7" singles: 'Clash City Rockers' is the faster version, 'The Magnificent Seven' the shorter one, and so on. From a purely historical point of view, *The Singles* demonstrates the incredible musical journey The Clash took in such a short period of time and it's hard to argue against anyone buying it to start their Clash collection.

CLASH ON BROADWAY

(USA November 1991, UK June 1994)

Disc 1: Janie Jones (demo)/Career Opportunities (demo)/White Riot/1977/I'm So Bored With the U.S.A./Hate & War/What's My Name/Deny/London's Burning/Protex Blue/Police & Thieves/48 Hours/Cheat/Garageland/Capital Radio One/Complete Control/Clash City Rockers/City of the Dead/Jail Guitar Doors/Prisoner/(White Man) In Hammersmith Palais/Pressure Drop/1-2 Crush On You/English Civil War (live)/I Fought The Law (live)

Disc 2: Safe European Home/Tommy Gun/Julie's In The Drug Squad/Stay Free/One Emotion/Groovy Times/Gates Of The West/Armagideon Time/London Calling/Brand New Cadillac/Rudie Can't Fail/The Guns Of Brixton/Spanish Bombs/Lost In The Supermarket/The Right Profile/The Card Cheat/Death Or Glory/Clampdown/ Train In Vain/Bankrobber

Disc 3: Police On My Back/The Magnificent Seven/The Leader/The Call Up/Somebody Got Murdered/Washington Bullets/Broadway/Lightning Strikes (Not Once But Twice) (live)/Every Little Bit Hurts/Stop The World/Midnight To Stevens/This Is Radio Clash/Cool Confusion/Red Angel Dragnet/Ghetto Defendant/Rock the Casbah/Should I Stay Or Should I Go/Straight To Hell/The Street Parade

Box set mania caught up with The Clash in America in 1991, by which time all hatchets had long been buried and the group were eager to see their music receive the stylish archive treatment already afforded lesser contemporaries. *Clash On Broadway* was the name of an intended movie by Don Letts around his filming of the Bond's Casino shows and surrounding mini-riots; as with so many Clash projects, it remained unfinished, its title resurrected here in honour of what The Clash consider their finest two weeks.

Furthering the focus on the box set's American audience, the accompanying booklet includes an essay by New York musician, writer and producer Lenny Kaye, and a lengthy excerpt from Lester Bangs' magnificent 1977 *NME* three-part story. There is no comparative essay by a British writer, and the all-American marketing focus left a familiar sour taste with British audiences when the set was finally released in the UK three years later. On the positive side, the booklet includes all manner of fond memories and insider info from the four Clash members and chief cohorts, as overseen by Kosmo Vinyl. Some of these stories may be apocryphal or exaggerated, but The Clash are a group of which The Myth is always preferable to The Truth. A separate booklet is included with the lyrics to all the songs on the three-CD set. (Originally issued in sturdy 12" x 6" packaging, Clash On Broadway is now sold in a standard jewel case.)

As with many box sets, *Clash On Broadway* is a combination of the widely familiar, the vaguely remembered and the previously unreleased – and in this case falls short of expectations by fleshing out the Greatest Hits format with a number of alternate versions. Overall, it's a non-essential purchase for anyone who has the studio albums or one of the double-CD compilations. For sheer size and attention to detail, however, it remains the ultimate Clash retrospective.

Notes: For reasons never explained (corporate Clash oversight?), 'Julie's Been Working For The Drug Squad' is re-titled 'Julie's In The

Drug Squad.' And in a throw-back to *London Calling*'s bonus 19th song, the third CD also includes one more track than the 18 listed: a slightly edited version of 'The Street Parade'. Both 'Rock The Casbah' and 'Should I Stay Or Should I Go' are the Mick Jones/Bob Clearmountain single remixes.

JANIE JONES/CAREER OPPORTUNITIES

There's no greater incentive for fans to buy a box set than to hear their heroes' first demo recordings. These two were part of a five song session recorded for Polydor Records at that label's London studio, in November 1976, as commissioned by A&R man Chris Parry. They're rendered of even greater historical interest by the presence of Guy Stevens as producer, whose involvement, at Bernie Rhodes' suggestion, was not without risk: Mick Jones had been pushed out of a group the last time they'd worked together (see *London Calling*) while Chris Parry, like everyone else in the business, was all too aware of Stevens' increased alcoholism and accompanying unreliability. In their *NME* interview with Tony Parsons, some of which can be heard on *The Story of The Clash Part 1*, Joe complained, complete with expletives, about producers "too pissed to work" and a "famous producer [who] said, 'You'd better pronounce the words.'" The former was definitely Stevens; the latter may have been engineer Vic Smith, who tried to rescue the three-day session as Stevens dissolved in front of them all. Either way, the end result was dissatisfying, the recordings lacking both the clarity and urgency of The Clash album, yet most profoundly let down by Strummer following orders and singing 'Career Opportunities' with exaggerated diction. Strummer learned his lesson from this, and for the next couple of years, would deliberately garble his words. (The complete session, with Terry Chimes on drums, is available on bootlegs; the other three songs recorded were 'White Riot', '1977' and 'London's Burning'.)

Footnote: The Clash claim they thought they were signing with Polydor up until the day of

the deal, when Bernie Rhodes sent them over to CBS instead. Chris Parry went on to sign, and Vic Smith to produce, The Jam, without any of the internecine battles that marked (but occasionally inspired) The Clash's career with CBS. For their part, of course, The Clash made up with Guy Stevens, hiring him to produce *London Calling*.

ENGLISH CIVIL WAR (live)/ I FOUGHT THE LAW (live)/ LIGHTNING STRIKES (NOT ONCE BUT TWICE) (live)

The Clash were always resistant to a live album, seeing it as part of the 'old way' of ripping off the fans. As a result, they recorded too few of their shows and when they did, the quality was often lacking. Hard though it seems to believe, these are the first *ever* official live Clash recordings. The sleeve notes date 'English Civil War' to 1979, when it's from the same show as 'I Fought The Law', the December 28, 1978 gig at London's Lyceum as recorded and filmed by Dave Mingay and Jack Hazan for the movie *Rude Boy*. The Clash had only recently introduced the latter Sonny Curtis song, and Strummer changed the words with typical Clash venom from "I left my baby" to "I killed my baby". He returned them to their original form for the later single release. If the recordings sound particularly tight, it may because The Clash returned to the studio to polish up at least the latter track for the movie, if not the first as well.

'Lightning Strikes' hails from the unfinished *Clash On Broadway* project, recorded at New York Bond's Casino in June (the 13th, almost certainly), 1981. It's of historical note for bringing the song back to the city that inspired it, though the live version, perhaps understandably, leans closer to rock than hip-hop. The Clash audience did not share their idols' infatuation with the new New York sound; hand-picked support acts Grandmaster Flash and The Furious 5, and The Treacherous 3, suffered heckling and hurled objects during the residency.

ONE EMOTION

Part of the Basing Street *Give 'Em Enough Rope* sessions, though it could as easily have been recorded inside a tin can. Certainly, it never got past the demo stage, and for good reason: the group started out composing a joke song about Roger Moore's acting range, then attempted to widen it into a more meaningful lyric, with Jones and Strummer sharing vocals. By that point it was over four minutes long and not going anywhere. Only for the archivists.

EVERY LITTLE BIT HURTS

(Ed Cobb)

An old soul song that Mick Jones would sing with future Pretender Chrissie Hynde during their pre-Clash attempt at making music together. After Hynde showed up at the *Sandinista!* sessions, Jones resurrected the song, but his voice is not strong enough to carry a soul ballad and for all Mickey Gallagher's keyboard playing, it sounds flat. It thereby has the unenviable distinction of being the only completed recording from the *Sandinista!* sessions not to make it onto the finished triple album *or* an accompanying B-side.

MIDNIGHT TO STEVENS

When Guy Stevens died in 1981, his lifestyle having caught up with him, Joe Strummer set about writing this tribute, a Mott The Hoople power ballad replica such as must have made Mick Jones sick with envy. Recorded at Ear Studios on to the Rolling Stones' mobile studio in London and then apparently forgotten about, it's the only previously unreleased song from *Clash On Broadway* worth seeking out, despite the unpolished mix. Strummer sings with honesty about Stevens' drink and drug problems, and ends with a poignant understanding of the producer's lifestyle and unfortunate destiny: "You've finished the booze and you run out of speed, but the wild side of life is the one that we need."

RED ANGEL DRAGNET/GHETTO DEFENDANT/STRAIGHT TO HELL

All three of these *Combat Rock* songs were edited down for length reasons in the mixing stage; strangely, in the case of the first two, *Clash On Broadway* presents not the original, longer versions, but yet tighter edits, as presumably were delivered to American radio. 'Red Angel Dragnet' loses part of Kosmo Vinyl's Travis Bickle speech; 'Ghetto Defendant' loses the last part of Allan Ginsberg's powerful poetry. (As compensation, the final, unreleased verse of 'Ghetto Defendant' is included in both the *Clash On Broadway* and *Combat Rock* lyric sheets.) 'Straight To Hell', on the other hand, is presented in its seven-minute unedited form, with an extra verse about New York's Alphabet City in the middle.

SUPER BLACK MARKET CLASH

(CD Release October 1993)

1977/ Listen/Jail Guitar Doors/City Of The Dead/The Prisoner/Pressure Drop/1-2 Crush On You/Groovy Times/Gates Of The West/Capital Radio Two/Time Is Tight/Justice Tonight/Kick It Over/Robber Dub/The Cool Out/Stop The World/The Magnificent Dance/Radio Clash/First Night Back In London/Long Time Jerk/Cool Confusion/Mustapha Dance

In October 1980, just before *Sandinista!* was unleashed, Epic Records in America released a 10" EP, *Black Market Clash*, to bring that country's listeners up to date on various British recordings unavailable in the States. Side 1 included 'Cheat' from *The Clash* album, and several early B-sides; Side 2 was strictly roots rock reggae, featuring 'Bankrobber' and the dub versions of both that song and 'Armagideon Time'. The album was eventually upgraded to full 12" vinyl and then in 1993, as CDs threatened to wipe vinyl off the shelves entirely, reworked by Kosmo Vinyl into the 21-track, 72 minute B-side bonanza *Super Black Market Clash*. The Clash thrived on the creative freedom afforded by B-sides, among which their remixes and dub versions are perhaps the most inspiring and innovative of all late Seventies/early Eighties groups. Throw in a couple of otherwise unavailable tracks and *Super Black Market Clash* is a frequently astounding album in its own right, a near

essential purchase right up there with the group's best studio sets. It's hard to understand why so many of these tracks were not included on the preceding "collector's compilation", *Clash On Broadway* - unless, perhaps, this project was in the works all along. All songs written by The Clash except where stated.

LISTEN
(Strummer-Jones)
The instrumental with which The Clash opened their set through most of 1976 and 1977, included on the *NME* Capital Radio 'EP' and made publicly available for the first and only time on this compilation. With its chord progressions and apparent choruses, 'Listen' sounds more like a complete Clash song waiting for lyrics than an intended instrumental. Full of punked-up energy, it reveals The Clash as far better musicians, far earlier on, that they generally liked to pretend.

PRESSURE DROP
(E. Hibbert)
The B-side to 'English Civil War' was the second attempt at recording this Toots & The Maytals song, after the earlier aborted effort with Lee Perry. It was worth getting right: falling somewhere between their earlier cover of 'Police & Thieves' and their own single '(White Man) In Hammersmith Palais', it's Clash punk-reggae at its most rhythmically powerful.

1-2 CRUSH ON YOU
(Strummer-Jones)
A Mick Jones composition dropped from The Clash set in 1976 as too overtly commercial and romantic for punk rock. By 1978, the group were confident enough of their standing to record it for the B-side of 'Tommy Gun'. The arrangement owes plenty both to Rhythm & Blues and Sixties punk; Jones' pure pop harmonies, a sax solo and a false ending all add to its harmless appeal.

TIME IS TIGHT
(Booker T. Jones)
The 1969 Booker T. & The M.G.'s

hit instrumental was recorded at the same time, same place as 'The Prisoner', 'Pressure Drop' and '1-2 Crush On You', but never found a B-side to call home. For the *Black Market Clash* 10", it was cleaned up by Bill Price at Wessex, after which it sounded as solid as any other Clash cover. The recording was bolstered by the guest appearance of the Attractions' Steve Naïve, widely considered one of the best piano players in the country. But for all that professionalism (and an unaccredited sax solo), it still has enough raw energy to be readily identifiable as The Clash.

JUSTICE TONIGHT/KICK IT OVER
(W. Williams/J. Mittoo)
The Clash had already proven themselves the best reggae cover band of the punk generation. With these two versions of 'Armagideon Time', segued together and released on the back of a 'London Calling' 12" single (their first), they also proved themselves masters of the dub mix. 'Justice Tonight' is the original recording drenched in effects and given a new voice-over by Strummer; 'Kick It Over' is more purely dub, stripping instruments away and allowing others to shine in the space provided. It all adds up to the best nine minutes of reggae The Clash ever recorded, mixed and dubbed up.

ROBBER DUB
(Strummer-Jones)
 Then again, Mikey Dread's dub mix of 'Bankrobber' gives it a close run for its money. The group's authentic approach to reggae was such that the audible difference between The Clash's dub mix of a Jamaican reggae song ('Justice Tonight'/'Kick It Over') and a Jamaican producer's dub of a Clash original ('Robber Dub') is negligible. 'Robber Dub' was intended for a Bankrobber 12" that was never released – partly because of CBS UK's persistent opposition to the single and maybe because it showed up on the *Black Market* 10" around the same time.

THE COOL OUT
A dub/remix of 'The Call Out' by Joe Strummer, Paul Simonon and Bernie Rhodes under the pseudonym Pepe Unidos. Absent the original track's military chants, giving focus to the rhythm and letting each instrument come forward when necessary, 'The Cool Out' is in many ways preferable to its original. Released on the American 12" of 'The Magnificent Seven'.

STOP THE WORLD
From the *Sandinista!* sessions, and released on the back of 'The Call Up' as part of a conceptual pair, Strummer viewing the post-nuclear nightmare from the midst of a purposefully painful kitchen-sink mix. For a B-side, that's fair enough, further proof that much of *Sandinista!* itself might have benefited from similar single distribution.

THE MAGNIFICENT DANCE
This instrumental dub/remix of 'The Magnificent Seven', released on that song's B-side, was already a big hit on influential black New York radio station WBLS when the group hit that city for its intended 'Magnificent Seven' night residency at Bond's Casino in Times Square in June '81. (After the Fire Department deemed that Bond's had oversold tickets, the residency was extended to 16 days and approximately 17 shows to cater to all the fans.) In comparison to some Clash dub versions, this is a relatively unfussy affair, which might have facilitated its appeal to radio; funky as anything, it proved such a perfect imitation of the New York sound of the era that many first-time listeners assumed The Clash were black.

History has determined Mick Jones as the Clash member most fascinated by New York dance culture, and most eager for the group to head in that musical direction. Yet for reasons never made clear, he was not involved in this mix, also credited to Pepe Unidos. Its success therefore indicates the extent to which The Clash could operate with one vision, even when absent a key part of its brain.

RADIO CLASH

Even the most obsessive Clash fans get confused by the proliferation of 'Radio Clash' mixes. *Super Black Market Clash* does not make it easier, labeling this recording as the A-side 'This Is Radio Clash' on the sleeve, and as both that *and* as the B-side 'Radio Clash' on the fold-out sleeve notes. It is, in fact, the latter – and those who have the 12" single will know it instead as the second track on the first side!

FIRST NIGHT BACK IN LONDON

The last four songs on *Super Black Market Clash* all saw release as B-sides to *Combat Rock* singles. As evidence of what went down at Ear Studios – Strummer's attempt to record an album straight to tape – 'First Night Back In London' justifies Mick Jones' insistence that they move instead to the previously proven Electric Ladyland. It's little more than a half song with vocals by Strummer in a nursery rhyme melody – when he raises his voice enough to sing, that is. Familiar lyrics about racism and the police and some atmospheric arrangements fail to raise it to the usual heights of a Clash B-side.

LONG TIME JERK

From the same sessions, recorded onto the Rolling Stones' mobile studio in London and later mixed by Mick Jones in New York. A stronger song than its predecessor, but the rockabilly rhythm is painfully simple, and the vocals again suffer from being spoken more than they're sung. First heard as 'Rock The Casbah''s B-side.

COOL CONFUSION

Recorded and mixed in New York during the *Combat Rock* sessions, and according to Kosmo Vinyl's sleeve notes, very nearly included on the finished album. Fortunately, there wasn't enough room and it was saved for the 'Should I Stay Or Should I Go' B-side. A non-song with no real melody or rhythm, 'Cool Confusion' has all the focus of a *Sandinista!* out-take.

MUSTAPHA DANCE

Super Black Market Clash ends in funky fine form with the wittily-named near-instrumental remix of and 12" addition to 'Rock The Casbah'. Not surprisingly, it hails from the same session with engineer Bob Clearmountain at which Mick Jones' remixed the A-side. That process served as a double vindication for The Clash guitarist, both in reclaiming 'Rock The Casbah' from Glyn Johns, and producing his own contemporary dance mix, after being absent from the process on 'The Magnificent Seven'. It proved a bitter victory: this solo studio production job would be his last with The Clash.

FROM HERE TO ETERNITY LIVE

(October 1999)

Complete Control/London's Burning/What's My Name/Clash City Rockers/Career Opportunities/(White Man) In Hammersmith Palais/Capital Radio/City Of The Dead/I Fought The Law/London Calling/Armagideon Time/Train In Vain/The Guns Of Brixton/The Magnificent Seven/Know Your Rights/Should I Stay Or Should I Go/Straight To Hell

That no live Clash album was released until fifteen years after the group's break-up indicates the extent to which they initially resisted the concept. And as mentioned above (*Clash On Broadway*), the group's dislike of the concert souvenir meant that too few of their shows were ever properly recorded. As a result, there is little on *From Here To Eternity* to surprise Clash fans: the album is effectively a cross-career Greatest Hits drawn from a handful of shows that were all either previously broadcast or otherwise familiar.

From Here To Eternity still succeeds (where so many live albums fail) in transferring the on-stage power of a great group to the relatively sterile format of the audio disc. Though it's never fully possible to replicate the visual dynamics, the listener can well imagine Mick Jones performing scissor kicks, Joe Strummer playing on his back, and Paul Simonon rushing around with his bass below his knees. Yet the scarcity (and quality?) of

live Clash recordings means that Topper Headon plays on barely half the album; eight of the 17 tracks hail from the period of Terry Chimes' reinstatement after *Combat Rock*. (Chimes is *still* the invisible man in Clash history; it's Headon who gets the full-page photo in the CD sleeve.) And while Mick Jones sang more than his fair share of lead with The Clash, he is featured here only on his two hit singles. To the credit of Bill Price, who mixed the album, *From Here To Eternity* could almost pass as one continuous concert, rather than a compendium of several shows over many years.

LONDON'S BURNING
April 30th, 1978, Victoria Park, Hackney, London.
From the memorable outdoor Rock Against Racism/Anti-Nazi League free concert in East London in front of over 50,000 people, many of whom had marched all the way from Trafalgar Square to protest the rise of the fascist right within Great Britain. The Tom Robinson Band closed out the concert (X-Ray Spex, Steel Pulse and Patrick Fitzgerald also played), but The Clash were clearly the star attraction. The performance was filmed by Dave Mingay and Jack Hazan and used in the movie *Rude Boy*.

WHAT'S MY NAME
July 27TH, 1978, Music Machine, London.
Also filmed for *Rude Boy*. At a time when The Clash were filling concert halls, they chose to end their Out On Parole tour with four nights at the long-standing Mornington Crescent club the Music Machine, which would later become New Romantic hang-out the Camden Palace. As befits the small room, it's an emphatic performance._

CITY OF THE DEAD/I FOUGHT THE LAW
December 28th, 1978, The Lyceum, London.
Again, this show was recorded only because it was filmed for *Rude Boy*, for which the latter song provided the finale. 'I Fought The Law' is the same recording, albeit a slightly

different mix, as that on *Clash On Broadway*. The *From Here To Eternity* sleeve notes admit that "some instrumental overdubs were recorded … at Air and Wessex Studios to repair technical deficiencies on the original live recordings" on all four of the above songs except 'City Of The Dead'. These technical deficiencies were likely the result of poor recording by the film-makerrs, but it's still a shame that the earliest official Clash live recordings can not lay claim to be fully "live".

CAPITAL RADIO/ARMAGIDEON TIME

February 18th, 1980, Lewisham Odeon, London.
As late as 1980, The Clash were still playing relatively small venues in their home city; this rare outing to south-east London was filmed by Don Letts as part of his promotional video for 'Bankrobber'. The inclusion of 'Capital Radio', with the coda elaborating on the musical idea formulated by *The Cost of Living*'s 'Capital Radio Two', would have been particularly poignant to the London audience. 'Armagideon Time' features Mikey Dread sharing vocals with Joe Strummer and indicates the group's ability to play dub reggae in a live capacity and to improvise in the process. Mickey Gallagher's impact is also evident.

COMPLETE CONTROL/TRAIN IN VAIN/THE GUNS OF BRIXTON

June 13th, 1981, Bonds Int. Casino, New York.
All filmed by Don Letts as part of the intended *Clash On Broadway* movie. The group have long reminisced on their two-week residency in Times Square as the high point of their career, and the recordings indeed reveal the band at its most emotionally intense and musically varied. From punk rock to disco funk to roots reggae, with three different vocalists in three different songs, it makes a listener long for the unexpurgated recordings of the whole show.

CLASH CITY ROCKERS/(WHITE MAN) IN HAMMERSMITH PALAIS/LONDON CALLING/THE MAGNIFICENT SEVEN/KNOW YOUR RIGHTS

September 7th, 1982, The Orpheum, Boston.

SHOULD I STAY OR SHOULD I GO/STRAIGHT TO HELL

September 8th, 1982, The Orpheum, Boston.
Most successful groups would have several of these professional radio broadcasts in their tape vaults; The Clash had only this pair of shows from their final tour, which were of course widely bootlegged over subsequent years. '(White Man)' includes a notable detour into The Skatalites 'Last Train To Skaville'; 'The Magnificent Seven' lacks the funk of the original recording and Strummer jokes about it being "twenty minutes long". Terry Chimes is professional throughout, but his drumming lacks the strength of Headon's surrounding performances: 'Straight To Hell' is largely propelled by a troublingly quiet kick drum. It's telling that while *From Here To Eternity* includes late career performances of all three classic Clash singles released immediately after their debut album, but that the second album itself, *Give 'Em Enough Rope,* remains unrepresented.

CAREER OPPORTUNITIES

October 13, 1982, Shea Stadium, New York.
The irony of performing a dole queue rant while playing an American baseball stadium as international superstars was not lost on The Clash, who seemed to revel in the moment as a telling justification for their own self-employment. (And though the humor is lost in the medium, they also had themselves filmed arriving and leaving in an open-top jeep.) The line "I don't want to die fighting in a Falklands Street" is a contemporary reference to the war in the South Atlantic between Britain and Argentina.

THE ESSENTIAL CLASH

(UK/USA, March 2003)

Disc 1: White Riot/1977/London's Burning/Complete Control/Clash City Rockers/I'm So Bored With The U.S.A./Career Opportunities/Hate & War/Cheat/Police & Thieves/Janie Jones/Garageland/Capital Radio One/(White Man) In Hammersmith Palais/English Civil War/Tommy Gun/Safe European Home/Julie's Been Working For The Drug Squad/Stay Free/Groovy Times/I Fought The Law

Disc 2: London Calling/The Guns Of Brixton/Clampdown/Rudie Can't Fail/Lost In The Supermarket/Jimmy Jazz/Train In Vain (Stand By Me)/Bankrobber/The Magnificent Seven/Ivan Meets G.I. Joe/Stop the World/Somebody Got Murdered/Street Parade/Broadway/This Is Radio Clash/ Ghetto Defendant/Rock The Casbah/ Straight To Hell/Should I Stay Or Should I Go/ This Is England

Released as part of Sony's ongoing series of "Essential" compilations, and serving as an audio companion to the DVD of the same name. Those looking for a bargain introduction to the Clash catalogue, but for more music than just the singles, have good reason to choose *The Essential Clash* over *The Story Of The Clash*. It makes maximum use of CD capacity, its 41 songs offering better value for money; it's in chronological order, apart from 'Complete Control' and 'Clash City Rockers' being placed ahead of

songs from *The Clash* album; and it dares to includes 'This Is England', making it the only compilation to acknowledge that The Clash continued after Mick Jones. The version of 'Clash City Rockers' is the slower recording; all other "singles" are the versions found on their original albums. The American release does not include '1977'.

LONDON CALLING 25th ANNIVERSARY EDITION

(Triple CD/DVD, UK/USA September 2004)

Disc 1: Original LP

Disc 2: The Vanilla Tapes. Hateful/Rudi Can't Fail/Paul's Tune/ I'm Not Down/4 Horsemen/Koka, Kola, Advertising & Cocaine/Death Or Glory/Lovers Rock/Lonesome Me/The Police Walked In 4 Jazz/Lost In The Supermarket/Up-Toon/Walking The Slidewalk/Where You Gonna Go/The Man In Me/Remote Control/Working And Waiting/Heart & Mind/Brand New Cadillac/London Calling/Revolution Rock

Disc 3: DVD – The Last Testament (The Making Of London Calling)

The demo tapes for *London Calling* were conveniently "discovered" in a box of old cassettes when Mick Jones moved house in March 2004 - just in time for a Silver Jubilee re-release of the album in September of the same year. Though this seems fortuitous beyond likely coincidence, Jones is probably right when he claims of the tapes, "They hadn't been heard since before the record was made." For that reason, they're of enormous historical interest – and occasionally, of qualitative merit too.

To recap the back story: after losing their Camden Town rehearsal rooms and finding new space at a place called Vanilla (36 Causton Street, off the Vauxhall Bridge Road in Pimlico), The Clash rediscovered their sense of adventure and began excitedly forming the songs that would become *London Calling*. Joe Strummer publicly entertained the idea of recording an album direct to tape at rehearsals, and after working up the new songs through May and June, The Clash brought in a Teac 4-track portastudio towards the end of June. For the next month, they recorded their renditions for daily cassettes, to which Mick Jones paid particularly close attention. (One day's worth of work was given to Johnny Green to hand to potential producer Guy Stevens; Green left them on the London Underground.)

According to Pat Gilbert's sleeve notes accompanying *The Vanilla Tapes*, Mick Jones identified some 37 different tracks for possible inclusion on this bonus CD, then whittled them down to this 67-minute, 21 song selection. They include, in some form or another, 15 of the 19 tracks ultimately featured on *London Calling*. (The four exceptions are 'Spanish Bombs', 'The Card Cheat', the final cover version 'Wrong Em Boyo' and, understandably given its legendary last minute addition, 'Train In Vain'.)

The Vanilla Tapes, even though they've gone unheard these 25 years, will be instantly familiar to anyone who's ever played in or listened to a band in a cheap rehearsal room. They are rough live recordings of works in progress, barely mixed, occasionally muffled, sometimes distorted and clearly copied over from time-worn cassettes. There are occasional doodles as are inevitable whenever band members are left unguarded in the studio, and a couple of instrumentals that could almost be from any band of the era jamming its way through another rehearsal day. Yet throughout, The Clash prove as tight musically in Vanilla as they would be at Wessex (perhaps even more so), which among other things, puts a lie to the notion that Simonon was still struggling as a bassist. The songs are, of course, free of overdubs – no brass, no keyboards, no additional percussion, all of which ensures a raw quality likely to be treasured by true fans. There are a handful of rarities and a few surprises. And a couple of the performances are so explosive that, demo cassette quality aside, they rival the final productions.

As well as a faithful single CD of the original *London Calling* double LP, The 25th Anniversary Edition comes with a DVD, which features as its main calling card a 40-minute documentary on the making of *London Calling*. Entitled *The Last Testament* as was the album's original working title, it's directed by Don Letts, and includes new interview material with Kosmo Vinyl along with further excerpts from the band interviews conducted for the *Westway To The World* documentary. (New interviews were shot with Jones and Simonon, but appear to have gone unused, perhaps because of continuity issues.) The documentary is a useful bonus, though it lacks the cohesion that made *Westway To The World* such addictive viewing, and adds little by way of revelations.

Perhaps more fascinating is the 16 minutes of black and white footage that shows the band in Wessex, with Guy Stevens in "direct psychic injection" mode, throwing chairs and ladders around the studio as so frequently claimed. However, it hadn't been known until now that said incident took place during a raw and unusable jam of 'Louie Louie', meaning that Stevens' method of apparent inspiration remains unproven to the wider public. Worse, his behaviour largely lacks humour: it's fairly safe to conclude that the producer is, at the very least, drunk on duty. The only other real footage of The Clash other than 'Louie Louie' is of Strummer recording vocals, and a blues jam featuring Headon on rhythm guitar, his girlfriend at his back, a roadie on drums and Strummer at the piano. All the same, the material has a grainy, archival magic. In modern days, with digital filming so inexpensive, camera crews routinely document "the making of the album"; here stands a rare case where such footage has been recovered long after the fact. Finally, the DVD also includes videos

associated with the album's singles: 'London Calling' (shot at Battersea Pier), and the superb live footage of 'Train In Vain' and 'Clampdown', from the 1980 Lewisham Odeon show. All three are also available on *The Essential Clash* DVD.

In contrast to the American bias of the *Clash On Broadway* box set, the packaging to *London Calling 25th Anniversary Edition* focuses on the group's roots in the British capital. An excellent essay by Tom Vague explains the background of (and the group's connection to) various London landmarks, while Pat Gilbert's notes on *The Vanilla Tapes* include quotes from Mick Jones. An early edition of The Armagideon Times, with brief handwritten explanations of certain *London Calling* tracks, is included, while the original Ray Lowry designed lyric sheet comes as a bonus fold-out.

The Vanilla Tapes break down as follows.

HATEFUL
As with the finished version, 'Hateful' finds The Clash at their most musically cohesive. Here it's played as an instrumental, providing an even firmer accent on the Bo Diddley beat.

RUDI CAN'T FAIL
With a slightly different spelling than the finished version, 'Rudi Can't Fail' is, like 'Hateful', minus its ultimate bells and whistles, allowing listeners to focus on the syncopation and the stereo separation of Jones' and Strummer's lead vocals.

PAUL'S SONG
It doesn't take a genius to figure this must be 'The Guns Of Brixton' in pre-titled form. Furthering the impression of a rudimentary recording, we hear a couple of failed introductions before Mick Jones suggests Topper lead off with a reggae drum roll. The performance is slower than the final recording, and it's absent the key chord changes that would mark the chorus. This may be because the song doesn't yet have

words; Jones flexes nicely on guitar, but the instrumental breaks down after just a couple of minutes for lack of development.

I'M NOT DOWN/4 HORSEMEN/KOKA, KOLA, ADVERTISING & COCAINE/DEATH OR GLORY/LOVER'S ROCK

Occasional altered song titles aside, these five are close to the final versions in structure and style, and provide the meat of the bonus CD. Interestingly, Mick Jones has the more endearing voice on *The Vanilla Tapes*. The guitarist liked to sing whereas Strummer preferred to shout and the former approach was more conducive to the confined environment of the rehearsal room. Strummer ultimately lowers his voice to somewhere between a rant and a drawl, and though he frequently drowns out the instruments (on a tightly performed but roughly recorded '4 Horsemen' and what would become 'Koka Kola'), the effect is to accentuate the words even more so than on the finished album. Strummer struggles with the melody on 'Lovers Rock', but he turns in a sterling performance on 'Death Or Glory' which, as per the finished album, proves to be one of this CD's most immediately accessible and simultaneously most enduring rockers.

LONESOME ME

The first of several cover versions, and a good indication of how wide The Clash would cast their net for inspiration. The Don Gibson country classic is very much a Mick Jones choice: he takes lead vocal, twangs through a Nashville guitar solo and even throws in some harmonica wails.

THE POLICE WALKED IN 4 JAZZ

An instantly recognisable instrumental version of what would become 'Jimmy Jazz', rendered all the more interesting for the presence of acoustic guitar, stereo separated from the electric. Jones' lead guitar solo is close to that which he'd record at Wessex.

LOST IN THE SUPERMARKET

Similar to the final recording in lyrics, melody, and guitar parts - and of special interest for hearing Mick Jones double-track his vocals in demo form. Topper Headon seems to be enjoying the opportunity to play a faux-disco rhythm.

UP-TOON (INSTRUMENTAL)

Though it has an entirely different title, this early instrumental version of 'The Right Profile' proves close in structure to the eventual Montgomery Clift tribute, and shows how carefully certain Clash songs were built before the lyrics were added. Presumably, the words came late: another instrumental version on Jones' cassettes carried the evocative but ultimately irrelevant title 'Canalside Walk'.

WALKIN' THE SLIDEWALK

An instrumental blues such as likely being performed across several dozen other London rehearsal rooms at that very moment. (And indeed, at *this* very moment.) Jones finds space for a fuzzy lead solo, but his skills do nothing to suggest the track ever had any real purpose.

WHERE YOU GONNA GO (SOWETO)

The first of two genuine Clash rarities on *The Vanilla Tapes*: self-composed songs that never made it on to record. One reason in this case may be the lyrics: whereas most of Strummer's vocals drown out the surrounding instruments, here he's singing in the background, as if still formulating the words. The other reason may be the rhythm which, with its slow reggae lilt, probably signified one West Indian arrangement too many for *London Calling*. Its unique status aside, the basic performance is only for true fanatics.

THE MAN IN ME

A Bob Dylan song, though being The Clash, they cover reggae group Matumbi's version. With 'Wrong 'Em Boyo' and 'Revolution Rock' making it onto *London Calling*, and 'Armagideon Time' on to the title track's B-side, 'The Man In Me' was likely abandoned as one reggae cover too many. As per its predecessor, the vocals are in the background, but Mick Jones' lead guitar lines, falling somewhere between his work on 'Police & Thieves' and a Mott The Hoople ballad, merit the song's inclusion.

REMOTE CONTROL

The only previously recorded Clash song on *The Vanilla Tapes* is, with typical Clash contrariness, the only one they had disowned. Mick Jones suggests on the sleeve notes that "we always liked the tune", though it should be noted that he wrote it. The group perhaps felt the need to reclaim 'Remote Control' from its negative "symbolic" connotations, and to toughen it up in the process, in which case they succeed: though poorly mixed with nearly inaudible vocals, it's a far more raucous and exciting version than the one that appeared on the Clash' debut album (and in much maligned 7" single form).

WORKING AND WAITING

An early instrumental version of 'Clampdown'. As with 'Death Or Glory', the Vanilla version benefits from the song's straight-forward rock arrangement: apart from vocals, this performance lacks for nothing. With the band at its tightest, and with the famous guitar riff placed center-mix at full volume, 'Working And Waiting' is the most explosive of all Vanilla recordings.

HEART AND MIND

The second unreleased Clash composition, with Strummer's vocals, an apparent examination of friendship and personalities, further upfront than on 'Where You Gonna Go'. 'Heart And Mind's ultimate disappearance from the Clash catalogue may be down to over-familiarity: those parts that don't sound like 'The Prisoner' are reminiscent of 'All The Young Punks' and 'Death Or Glory'. A coda of The 101ers minor hit 'Keys To Your Heart' furthers the notion of insider plagiarism.

BRAND NEW CADILLAC/LONDON CALLING/REVOLUTION ROCK

The Vanilla Tapes close out with two of *London Calling*'s covers sandwiching the title track. 'Brand New Cadillac' is tight but lacks the fire of the Stevens-produced version. 'London Calling' is still unformed, which probably explains its placement so late in the CD, and Strummer's drawled vocals are so off-key it almost sounds like Simonon at the microphone instead. The recording is of major historical interest primarily for its markedly different lyrics, about the youth cults that dominated Britain back in 1979. (Though they provide a more specific commentary than Strummer's ultimate verses, their inclusion in the finished version would have forever dated the song to a moment in time.) 'Revolution Rock' is an affectionate instrumental version that appears to have gone through a rudimentary dub mix on the four-track: some instruments drop out and others are suddenly muffled. All four members are clearly enjoying the work-out and with Headon at his finest, 'Revolution Rock' ends *The Vanilla Tapes* in optimistic form. This time round, there is no hidden track.

THE SINGLES (BOX SET)

CD BOX SET, 2006

Disc 1: Whit Riot/1977
Disc 2: Listen (Edit)/Interview With The Clash On The Circle Line (Part One)/Interview With The Clash On The Cirlce Line (Part Two)/Capitol Radio One
Disc 3: Remote Control/London's Burning (Live)/London's Burning
Disc 4: Complete Control/City Of The Dead
Disc 5: Clash City Rockers/Jail Guitar Doors
Disc 6: (White Man) In Hammersmith Palais/The Prisoner
Disc 7: Tommy Gun/1-2 Crush On You
Disc 8: English Civil War (Johnny Comes Marching Home)/Pressure Drop
Disc 9: I Fought The Law/Groovy Times/Gates Of The West/Capital Radio Two
Disc 10: London Calling/Armagideon Time/Justice Tonight/Kick It Over/Clampdown/The Card Cheat/Lost In The Supermarket
Disc 11: BankRobber/Rockers Galore...UK Tour/Rudie Can't Fail/Train In Vain
Disc 12: The Call Up/Stop The World
Disc 13: Hitsville UK/Radio One/Police On My Back/Somebody Got Murdered
Disc 14: The Magnificent Seven (Edit)/The Magnificent Dance (Edit)/Lightening Strikes (Not Once But Twice)/One More Time/One More Dub/The Cool Out/The Magnificent Seven (12' Version)/The Magnificent Dance (12' Version)
Disc 15: This Radio Clash/Radio Clash/Outside Broadcast/Radio 5
Disc 16: Know Your Rights/First Night Back In London
Disc 17: Rock The Casbah/Long Time Jerk/Mustapha Dance/Red Angel Dragnet/Overpowered By Funk
Disc 18: Should I Stay Or Should I Go/Straight To Hell (Edited Version)/Inoculated City/Cool Confusion
Disc 19: This Is England/Do It Now/Sex Mad Roar

The Clash's reputation as a singles band *par excellence* was given its true due when Sony packaged every one of their 19 UK 7" and 12" releases into a lavish replica CD box set. While the collection is arguably only for completists, it would also serve as an excellent starting point for those with sufficiently deep pockets: The Clash are at their best when listened to in the natural progression of their single statements, especially those that appeared in between albums (which was many of them). The ample space of the compact disc format allows for the vagaries of different international B-sides to be gathered together on every individual CD. In a few cases, this dissipates from the original message, but having an eight-track CD to celebrate 'The Magnificent Seven' certainly makes much more sense than trying to keep track of the various vinyl components from 1981. The decision to include 'This Is England,' following its inclusion on *The Essential Clash* in 2003, suggests that it has been officially rehabilitated into the Clash discography.

The Singles Box Set is further enhanced by the use of original art work and labels and a series of reminiscences and testimonials from a wide range of artistic luminaries including Pete Townshend, Mike D, Shane MacGowan, Steve Jones, Damon Albarn, Bobby Gillespie, Bernard Sumner, Nick Hornby and Danny Boyle.

LIVE AT SHEA STADIUM

CD, 2008

Tracks: London Calling/Police On My Back/The Guns of Brixton/Tommy Gun/Magnificent 7/Armagideon Time/Magnificent 7 (Return)/Rock The Casbah/Train In Vain/Career Opportunities/Spanish Bombs/Clampdown/English Civil War/Should I Stay Or Should I Go/I Fought The Law

If any Clash appearance was likely to be unearthed and released as a stand-alone live album, it was always bound to be New York's Shea Stadium 1982, where the group opened for The Who. It can be seen, at least from the record company perspective, as the moment when The Clash most evidentally "arrived" in America, and yet coming as late as it does in the band's short reign, allows for complete catalogue coverage. In addition, the top-quality sound mixing and equally professional filming avoids the audio and visual pitfalls associated with earlier archived concerts. Whether Shea Stadium captured the group at their on-stage *best* is a matter of greater debate: Topper Headon had already been fired for heroin addiction (Terry Chimes, the group's original drummer, returned for the final tours), and Mick Jones would follow within the year. It would be more accurate to call it a swan song than a critical peak.

Still, the band put in a remarkably solid, and impressively varied set, on this, the third of the three Shea shows, October 13 1982. The obvious American crowd-pleasers are all present and correct - 'Tommy Gun,' 'Clampdown,' 'Rock The Casbah,' 'London Calling,' 'English Civil War,' and a finale of 'I Fought The Law'. But it remains the Clash's greatest achievement that they were able to succeed across so many different genres, and credit should be given for the unapologetic promotion (against what may have been audience resistance) of Paul Simonon singing 'The Guns Of Brixton,' and Mick Jones taking on Eddie Grant's 'Police On My Back' as well as his own disco classic (and the Clash's only previous top 40 hit), 'Train In Vain'. Most impressive of all is the early live journey "to New York, Jamaica and back" via a medley of 'The Magnificent Seven' and the classic 'London Calling' B-side 'Armagideon Time'. Given that the concert is now a live souvenir for Clash fans worldwide, we may forgive Strummer for failing to note that the crowd was already in New York at the time.

If there's a surprise, it's that only two songs from *Combat Rock*, at the time sailing high in the American charts, were included in the hour-long set. The decision to perform 'Career Opportunities' was always intended as a deliberately ironic statement on how far the group had traveled, in all senses, since its initial, lo-fi recording, back in 1977 – although as an additional attempt to reclaim the song from its disastrous re-interpretation on *Sandanista!*, it also succeeds, emphatically.

PART III
FILMS, DVDS
COMPILATIO

VIDEO

RUDE BOY

(U.S. VHS, UK DVD/VHS, 1980)

The full-length feature *Rude Boy* is not an official Clash movie, and it's all the better because of it. In 1977, thirty-something directors/producers Jack Hazan and Dave Mingay began filming street confrontations between the National Front and its opponents, and soon moved in on the punk movement, where socialist and fascist recruiters alike were competing for the young audience's allegiance. Seizing on a Brixton-based Clash fan, Ray Gange, as an appropriate everyman around which to create some form of plot, Hazan and Mingay approached Bernie Rhodes for permission to film The Clash in concert and set up encounters between Gange and the band; Rhodes embraced the idea as cinematic embodiment of his Situationist beliefs and quickly gave the film-makers a virtual carte blanche.

The Buzzy crew filmed The Clash several times in concert through 1978 - inadvertently ensuring that, at a time when movie-making was prohibitively expensive for young groups, this most explosive of punk bands was extensively documented. Among the concerts were a couple of truly memorable, typically chaotic events: the Rock Against Racism/Anti-Nazi League festival in London's Victoria Park, in front of over 50,000 people; and the last ever show at the Glasgow Apollo, where the bouncers exacted vicious vengeance on all the young punks who'd ever dared demand the right to enjoy themselves.

The former event shows The Clash at their most forcefully chaotic. Road manager Johnny Green reacts swiftly (and with menace) when supposed headliners The Tom Robinson Band pull the plugs on The Clash's set, after which Sham 69's Jimmy Pursey gatecrashes the party to ruin 'White Riot', and Ray Gange assumes the role of MC at the show's conclusion. The latter concert shows The Clash out of their depth as the bouncers beat the fans with fists and boots. Much like Mick Jagger at Altamont, Strummer seems genuinely scared as he launches into the provocative finale of 'White Riot', while Jones, like Jagger's guitar-playing partner Keith Richards at Altamont, maintains his cool. Crucially, neither member gets physically involved, and the brutal scene, as much as any off-stage dialogue, reveals the permanent gulf between performer and punter, even amongst the punks. Thankfully, *unlike* Altamont, no one gets killed.

Strummer and Simonon were arrested right after the Glasgow concert (Strummer for throwing a bottle at a wall in frustration; Simonon for coming to his aid); they are shown emerging from the police station the following morning, laughing at the absurdity of it all. Likewise, the camera crew follow Simonon and Headon's regular visits to Clerkenwell Crown Court as the 'Guns On The Roof' incident drags on to its inconsequential conclusion. The cameras are also there at Basing Street for the *Give 'Em Enough Rope* sessions: Joe is shown singing 'All The Young Punks' and Mick what appears to be the final vocal for 'Stay Free', the camera coming so close we can hear their deep breathing. (Unfortunately, there's no sight of Sandy Pearlman at work.)

Ray Gange proves a fascinating case study, if a terrible actor. He claims unemployment but works in a sex shop; he declares a determination to break out of his rut but when offered a chance to roadie for The

Clash, squanders it through laziness and heavy drinking. Most disturbingly, but not atypically, he's a Clash fan whose politics lean increasingly to the extreme right. There's a fascinating, staged (but not necessarily scripted) scene in Brixton pub The Railway where Gange declares his desire to have "a lot of money, and a country mansion, and servants." Strummer, who at public school would have been exposed to the offspring of the upper classes, tries to convince Gange that "There's nothing at the end of that road, no human life or nothing." The irony, of course, is that Strummer has the wits to make money, should he want to; Gange can only dream.

A late movie scene in a rehearsal room brings them back together. Gange, drinking Special Brew (and apparently unaware of his increasingly pathetic on-screen persona) complains that The Clash should stop mixing music and politics; a clear-headed Strummer plays 'Let The Good Times Roll' with a wry smile on his face as Gange slouches in a stupor round the room.

As well as the live Clash footage, the off-stage scenes, and the barely scripted/cinema verité aspects involving central character Gange, there's a not fully effective subplot about black Brixton pickpockets, their white police surveillance teams, their eventual arrests and possibly forced confessions. The final element in the movie is pure documentary: odious National Front spokesmen at the peak of their publicly permitted race-baiting, naïve policemen contentedly linking arms to protect the fascists as they march, Margaret Thatcher playing on the politics of fear at a Conservative conference, and the same party leader closing out the movie as she arrives at Downing Street in May 1979 as Prime Minister. It's no coincidence that the final Clash song, from The Lyceum in December 1978, is 'I Fought The Law' (which would be released as a single the month of the British election). Mingay and Hazan appear to believe that the forces of real power – the police, the bouncers, the politicians – have

won out over the well-meaning but disorganised musicians and their once optimistic punk rock rebellion. If Gange is any example, *Rude Boy* appears to be stating, The Clash have failed to show even their closest fans the path of true righteousness.

By the time *Rude Boy* had been edited, The Clash had sacked Bernie Rhodes – and his successor, Caroline Coon, who appears frequently in the movie – and their new managers, Andrew King and Peter Jenner, tried to stop the film from being released, apparently at the group's own request. But Rhodes had signed a contract with Buzzy and the band had banked an advance: the threats of legal action remained just that. The Clash ultimately delivered the song 'Rudie Can't Fail' for the movie, and polished up certain live tracks for the final edit. Released in early 1980, *Rude Boy* fared poorly at the British box office, partly because of bad reviews and partly because of The Clash's verbal opposition; it was more successful in Europe and America. For all its evident flaws in terms of structure, editing and, most flagrantly, acting, history has served *Rude Boy* well. There is surely no more interesting a movie about the politics of punk rock in late Seventies Great Britain. And there is certainly no better document of The Clash at their most combustible.

WESTWAY TO THE WORLD

(DVD/VHS, 2001)

The one artifact that best explains The Clash is not an audio recording, but the documentary *Westway To The World*. Don Letts' film draws on the customary archive footage, all of which is well worth watching, but what elevates the movie to essential viewing status is the powerful reflective presence of the individual band members. Joe, Mick, Paul and Topper, along with Tony Chimes, Bill Price, Johnny Green and Tony Parsons all discuss the old days from the varying vantage points of their middle-aged maturity, and with a frequently painful honesty.

This is not to suggest that everyone is always telling the truth: there are plenty of statistical exaggerations, anecdotal myths and apocryphal legends. And as much is revealed about The Clash by what they leave out of the story – the continuation of the group after Mick Jones, for notable example – as by what they include. But it's clear that the musicians have all come to terms with their individual roles in the collective Clash impact, which enables them to approach the past with great affection. More than anything, *Westway To The World* captures the underlying humour within The Clash as was often lost amidst the musical noise during their time together. Joe describes Mick Jones late in Clash life as "like Elizabeth Taylor in a filthy mood", while for his part Mick defends *Sandinista!* as "a record for people who were

on oil rigs or arctic stations and weren't able to get to the record stores regularly."

Don Letts, who like Mick Jones attended a South London grammar school in the early Seventies, gets some front-of-camera credit from Joe Strummer for bringing reggae to punks in his role as The Roxy's DJ. The director otherwise stays behind the scenes, splicing the interviews (conducted by Mal Peachey) with footage of various live shows, TV clips and occasional news footage. Most of this material is available in extended form on *The Essential Clash* DVD, but shots from The Roxy, brief images of The Clash rehearsing in 1976, and footage of the *Top Of The Pops*' all-girl dance team Pans People "interpreting" 'Bankrobber' are all priceless.

Westway To The World was made in 2000, the same year as Julien Temple's documentary film on The Sex Pistols, *The Filth And The Fury*. In each case, the director had been around his subject since their early days, and each group's members were interviewed individually, in close-up, at a point in their lives where they could afford to be brutally honest about the past. And as with John Lydon in *The Filth And The Fury*, the front man steals the show. Joe Strummer *owns Westway To The World*: his emotional honesty, physical energy and intellectual quest continually propels the footage forward. Unlike *The Filth And The Fury*, however, *Westway To The World* did not play in cinemas; after being shown in edited form on various television channels as additional promotion for the newly revamped Clash back catalogue, it went straight to a home release. It was, however, recognised for its merits by the most unlikely of organisations: in 2002, *Westway To The World* won Don Letts a Grammy.

That said, Letts allows unforgivable errors. The Victoria Park concert is dated May 1977 when it was in April 1978, and the Guns on the Roof incident is annotated as January 1977 (long before lead culprit Headon joined the band) when it was in fact March 1978. Peachey's back cover notes talk of The Clash playing Shea Stadium in 1981 and Bond's in 1982, when it was the other way round, and perpetuates the belief that *Combat Rock* went top five in America, when it was but a Top 10 album. That claim is further exaggerated by Strummer insisting on camera, "It was unheard of for us, our placings had been 198, lower than that." (*London Calling* and *Sandinista!* had, in fact, both gone Top 30 in the States.)

But for a band so wrapped up in its own mythology, dates and chart positions don't have to be accurate for a documentary to be truthful. The group's desire to finally set the record straight is most apparent as the individual members reflect either on being ousted from the band, or their role in the ousting.

Topper Headon, looking thin and worn and much older than the others, says sorry as only a drug addict can: "I'd like to apologise to them for letting the side down, for going off the rails, but if it happened again, I'd probably do the same thing."

Mick Jones all but admits he deserved to be sacked: "I didn't know personally about self control... You wish you knew what you know now."

And Joe Strummer seems furious at himself for sacking either of the above. "If it works, do whatever you have to do to bring it forward, but don't mess with it. We learned that *bitterly*."

Only Paul Simonon, as stolid and relaxed as ever, seems fully satisfied by the whole Clash adventure. "We did our job and that's the story and now we're gone. And that's it. That suits me fine." They are the last words we hear.

The DVD comes complete with extra interview material with the four primary members that is revealing in its own right. There's also 22 minutes of *Clash On Broadway* footage shot by Don Letts during the Bond's residency in 1981. "The film of that event was destroyed," reads the label sleeve. "This salvaged copy is the only record." So we are told.

THE ESSENTIAL CLASH

(DVD, 2003)

Released in synch with the double audio CD of the same name, *The Essential Clash* gathers all the available promo videos, rare old footage and enough live material to merit the title. (In the process, it replaces the former eight-song VHS-only release, *This Is Video Clash.*)

Most of it is directed by Don Letts. His opening *Clash On Broadway* "trailer" is a misnomer considering the movie was never released, but the ten minute clip captures the internal excitement and occasional external mayhem that surrounded the group's concerts at Bond's in New York in June 1981. It also includes some live footage of 'London Calling' and 'This Is Radio Clash', while 'Complete Control' (the same recording as appeared on *From Here To Eternity*) is accompanied by a visual montage. 'Clampdown' and 'Train In Vain' are both from the 1980 Lewisham Odeon gig that spawned other recordings for the live album; these performances show The Clash at their finest and suggests that any other footage or audio recordings as exist should be released as soon as possible. 'Should I Stay Or Should I Go' and 'Career Opportunities' hail from Shea Stadium in October 1982; the latter is the same recording as on the live album. Sartorial elegance aside, they show The Clash as having lost none of their impact in the stadium format.

Of the more conventional promo clips, 'London Calling' was filmed in the rain at Battersea Pier, and exudes a certain Clash cool. 'Bankrobber' shows the group recording the song in the studio, and later at Lewisham Odeon, with Mikey Dread and Mickey Gallagher as part of an extended line-up. A staged bank robbery in Lewisham by road crew members The Baker and Johnny Green supplies a farcical element that was typical of the era's videos. 'The Call Up''s preposterous costumes and setting render what was already a "difficult" single yet more indigestible. 'Rock The Casbah' epitomises the early days of MTV but, thanks to the group's powerfully mimed performance and the comic interaction between the Sheik and the Jew, it holds up better than so many other artifacts from that era.

Of the pre-Letts material, 'Tommy Gun' is lip-synched on stage, the camera getting closer to Strummer's dental decay than advisable. 'White Riot' shows up both in the 'Tracklisting' and amongst the 'Special Features', where it is accompanied by 'London's Burning' and '1977' from the same performance. The DVD cover states that this 'Promo Footage' is from 1976, but Marcus Gray's Clash biography *The Last Gang In Town* dates it to Dunstable in the spring of 1977. Anyone still confused as to why The Clash were elevated to the position of Great Punk Hope in 1977 need only watch these brief clips: performing live on a rehearsal room stage, direct to a roving camera, The Clash are simply phenomenal. CBS used the 'London's Burning' recording as the "live" B-side for 'Remote Control'.

Of equal historic note is the group's first televised interview, with Janet Street Porter on the *London Weekend Show* in 1976. The band projects the requisite punk combination of anger and aloofness, and if Mick Jones sounds hypocritical in retrospect, criticising hippies for smoking "too much dope", it's worth considering how galvanising the sight of the three paint-splattered musical upstarts would have seemed to young viewers at the time. Rounding out the raw material is the same clip of 'I Fought The Law' from The Lyceum 1978, as closed out *Rude Boy*.

All this is enough to merit *The Essential Clash* its title. But the DVD also includes, for the first time in any way, shape or form, the silent movie *Hell W10*, written and directed by Joe Strummer in early 1983 when The Clash were meant to be taking a much-needed holiday. Clash mythology can be particularly imaginative, and the assurance that the film had been considered lost until "a very rough copy was found by a pair of fans at a car boot sale" must be taken with a large dose of salt at hand.

No worries. It's easy to see why the movie was never finished, and it's equally obvious why it should have been released twenty years later. *Hell W10* looks like exactly what it was: a rock star's attempt to make a silent gangster movie, somewhere between *The Keystone Cops* and *The Harder They Come*. To this end, Strummer uses band mates and friends as cast, their flats and offices as interior locations, and the local streets of Notting Hill

and Ladbroke Grove – the Portobello Road in particular – for exterior shots. The hour-long film, which only struggles to hold viewer attention for its lack of dialogue, stars Paul Simonon in a predictable 'Johnny Too Bad' role as Earl, Mick Jones as his smartly dressed gangland leader nemesis Socrates, and associates ranging from Kosmo Vinyl to Pennie Smith as various cohorts and law enforcement. (Strummer briefly steps in front of camera as a moustache'd policeman.) The plot, such as we can follow it, revolves around stolen porn tapes and various gangland vendettas, and ends with a bloody shoot-out under The Westway. From a film aficionado's point of view, Hell W10 is rankly amateur, but its self-effacing comedy is extremely endearing, not least because it's the last time The Clash are seen on tape enjoying each other's company. The soundtrack to *Hell W10* has been added especially for the DVD, comprising vaguely appropriate songs from *Sandinista!* - including ten instrumental versions never before released. A previously unseen home Clash movie with a bonus album. It's hard to raise an objection.

THE CLASH LIVE - REVOLUTION ROCK

DVD, 2008

It had long been a source of frustration for Clash fans that live visual recordings had been released haphazardly, if at all. The footage included in *Rude Boy, Westway To The World* and the *Essential Clash* only ever hinted at the depth of material fans had been passing around for years on VHS and DVD bootlegs over the years. The *From Here To Eternity* live CD, meanwhile (see review) proved equally frustrating for the fact that so much of it hailed from the later, post-Headon period. Some credit is due, then, for this 2008 Don Letts directorial attempt to compile a chronological concert 'Best Of,' even though *far* too much of it has been gathered up before, and it comes with an annoying default voice-over that suggests pretensions to being a documentary rather than a compilation in its own right.

Taken chronologically, the highlights can be broken down into two distinct categories. The 1970s clips come exclusively from Europe, including a riveting performance in Manchester for Granada TV's ground-breaking show *So It Goes* in November 1977 (though sadly not the scene that shows Strummer, having endured a painful backwards fall onto the drum riser at the end of 'What's My Name', sings 'Garageland' from the floor), and a show in Germany the same year. Excellent footage from the Glasgow Apollo and the Hackney Park Rock Against Racism carnival in 1978, and from the

London Lyceum in 1979, will all be familiar to those who own a copy of *Rude Boy*; 'Train In Vain' from Lewisham Odeon 1980 is included on *The Essential Clash* DVD.

Reflecting the Clash's increasing international appeal, the filming then skips overseas for the duration. Most of it emanates comes from New York, and some of it is sensational: the obligatory and, frankly, overused footage of 'Should I Stay Or Should I Go' from Shea Stadium in 1982 - is tempered in part by 'London Calling' from Bonds in 1981 but more so by the inclusion of a taut performance of 'The Guns of Brixton' from Fridays in 1980, and in particular, by the group's incendiary appearance on the Tom Snyder show in the midst of the 1981 Bonds run. There's also a welcome if poorly shot clip from Tokyo 1982, and a performance of 'Know Your Rights' from the Us Festival in May 1983, the last ever appearance of the Clash as they truly mattered. The bonus feature interviews from 1981 and 1982 New York TV shows (the second of which is inaccurately dated on the DVD) are interesting to see the American media perspective.

Assuming the footage exists (and the Us Festival has long done the rounds in its entirety), any one of these concerts might yet justify a DVD release on its own, along with others that have yet to be officially unveiled. In the meantime, *Revolution Rock* tries its best. But *Westway To The World*, even though presented as a documentary, does better.

TRACKLISTING: 1. Complete Control; 2. I Fought The Law (London Lyceum '79); 3. Police & Thieves (Munich '77); 4. What's My Name (Manchester Elizabethan Suite '77) - previously unreleased; 5. Capitol Radio One (Manchester Elizabethan Suite '77) - previously unreleased; 6. White Riot; 7. I'm So Bored With The U.S.A (Manchester Apollo '78) - previously unreleased; 8. London's Burning (London Victoria Park '78); 9. 1977; 10. (White Man) In Hammersmith Palais (Glasgow Apollo '78); 11. Tommy Gun; 12. Safe European Home (London Music Machine '78); 13. London Calling (Bonds International Casino '81) (inc on Westway to the World); 14. Clampdown (Lewisham Odeon '80); 15. The Guns Of Brixton (Fridays '80) - previously unreleased; 16. Train In Vain (Lewisham Odeon '80); 17. This Is Radio Clash (Tomorrow Show With Tom Snyder '81) - previously unreleased; 18. The Magnificent Seven (Tomorrow Show With Tom Snyder '81) - previously unreleased; 19. Brand New Cadillac (Tokyo Sun Plaza Hall '82) - previously unreleased; 20. Should I Stay Or Should I Go (Shea Stadium '82); 21. Know Your Rights (US Festival '83) - previously unreleased; 22. Career Opportunities (Shea Stadium '82)

PART IV

POST-CLASH SOLO CAREERS

Mick Jones' initial reaction to getting sacked from The Clash was to challenge the very concept: as the group's founding member, co-songwriter and main in-house producer, surely he had as strong a claim to the band as anyone? To this end, he quickly set about hiring Nicky Headon to form a rival Clash. As it turned out, and despite his best efforts, the drummer's drug addiction was beyond repair at the time, and so, after putting an (ultimately ineffective) injunction on The Clash's name and (temporarily effective) freeze on their assets, he set about establishing a new group. Jones immediately pulled off a personnel coup when he convinced The Clash's long standing video director, Don Letts, to join him on special effects and verbal toasting. Jones furthered his credentials with former Basement 5 bassist Leo Williams, hired Greg Roberts on drums and rounded out what he hoped would be a multi-media group with Dan Donovan on keyboards and "photography". He called the band Big Audio Dynamite, B.A.D. for short.

Big Audio Dynamite introduced themselves to the British public with the single 'The Bottom Line', released at the same time, in September 1985, as The Clash "comeback" single 'This Is England'. A spaghetti western call to "the dance of economic decline" as played by synthesizers, funk bass, programmed drum beats and guitars - a mix for which Jones' frail voice was ideally suited – it was so unusual that it failed to chart. (An extended 12" mix, however, with chanted group vocals and wide use of sound effects, immediately provoked admiration in the dance clubs.) But when the debut album *This Is Big Audio Dynamite* saw UK release in November 1985 up against *Cut The Crap*, there was no doubt which was the better record, little subsequent debate as to which would be the more commercially successful, and no long term question about which was the more influential. *This Is Big Audio Dynamite* was arguably the first album to incorporate electronic sampling, hip-hop beats, dub vibes, dance grooves and guitar rock and present them all, if in somewhat

overdressed cowboy clothing, as an entirely natural combination. At a time when most exciting new music was emanating from America (and that had included *Combat Rock*), the fact that B.A.D. were British, recording in London (Jones having returned to West London studios), proved no small source of national musical pride. Subsequent singles 'Medicine Show' and 'E=MC2' both charted in the UK, the latter peaking at number 11, as high as 'London Calling', the biggest hit by The Clash.

In getting sacked from The Clash, Mick Jones had been painted as habitually unpunctual, and something of a time-waster in the studio. If so, he quickly learned his lesson: he was recording B.A.D.'s second album while the first was still making its presence felt in the clubs. This time he had company: a remorseful Joe Strummer, who had by now broken up The Clash, not least in awareness that B.A.D. was making the more exciting music. To Jones' eternal credit, he welcomed Strummer back as a friend and, when his former Clash partner apparently proved unwilling to take his leave, gave him several co-songwriting credits and a Co-Production credit. It's hard to ascertain Strummer's contribution in these roles, as *No. 10, Upping St.* continued very much along the lines of its predecessor. In fact, most listeners agree that it's a weaker album than the B.A.D. debut, which suggests that Jones worked better on his new musical vision unencumbered by former Clash members. The 'Strummer-Jones' partnership reintroduced itself as authors of 'Beyond The Pale', 'Sightsee M.C!' and the single 'V. Thirteen'. (The Jones-Letts composition 'C'mon Every Beatbox' was the album's first single.)

By the time of B.A.D.'s third album *Tighten Up Vol. 88*, named in homage to ska label Trojan's *Tighten Up* series, Paul Simonon was on board as cover artist, depicting a colourful sound system party against the Clash-mythologised backdrop of Westway tower blocks. It was an apt sleeve, for that summer, 1988, a new British dance scene exploded, drawing less on New York hip-hop than the house music sounds of Chicago and the techno of Detroit. All of a sudden, white kids were dancing all night at "raves" (a successor to the warehouse parties such as B.A.D. members had regularly attended), buying samplers, playing synthesizers and taking the drug ecstasy in such numbers that even football hooligans turned into temporary arbiters of peace and love. As with punk a decade earlier, Mick Jones was operating at the very heart of a new British street movement, though *Tighten Up* didn't fully absorb the new sound, and in offering only 'Just Play Music' as a viable single, is considered a weak album by the group's generally high standards.

Unfortunately, Jones chose that moment in time – or rather, it chose him - to catch chickenpox from his four-year-old daughter, and he very nearly died from the disease. Yet despite going into a coma and spending months in recuperation, Jones rushed back into recording as his form of convalescence. With Bill Price on board as co-producer, he had the lengthy *Megatop Phoenix* in the stores by the autumn of 1989. It embraced rave culture and acid house without abandoning B.A.D.'s unique sound: the single 'Contact' combined a house-driven piano line *and* a sample from The Who's 'I Can't Explain', and became an enormous club hit in America. Mick's close encounter with death rendered the various shout-outs on the inner sleeve that much more emotionally sincere – especially the one to his nan, Stella, who died that year.

Mutiny in the ranks saw Jones' compadres leave him to form their own (less successful) bands. (Dan Donovan made the news in his own right by becoming the first in a succession of rock star husbands of Eighth Wonder singer and occasional film actress Patsy Kensit.) Undeterred as always, Jones formed Big Audio Dynamite II, recruiting drummer Chris Kavanagh from his old friend Tony James' band Sigue Sigue Sputnik, along with Gary Stonadge on bass and Nick Hawkins on guitar. The new B.A.D. confused fans with the limited edition album *Kool-Aid*,

before revamping it in 1991 and renaming it after another of its songs, *The Globe*. Co-produced with André Shapps, *The Globe* contains some of Jones' finest work with or without The Clash, including the title track (named for a Notting Hill watering hole) and the single 'Rush' (this one incorporating a sample from The Who's 'Baba O'Riley'). B.A.D. toured the States alongside Public Image Ltd, embarrassing John Lydon's punk nostalgia trip in the process. Yet even as 'Rush' impressively scaled the American top 40, B.A.D.'s influence went further: EMF and Jesus Jones, who with their roving on-stage synth players, crisp hip-hop beats and Stussy clothing, could hardly deny their debt to B.A.D., held the top two chart positions in America around the same time.

It proved to be B.A.D.'s zenith. Jones finally slowed his daunting pace of recording, and by the time the group re-emerged, now as Big Audio, with *Higher Power* in 1994, the music scene had moved on. The days of rave and indie dance had fallen by the wayside, and Jones was suddenly out of step with the times – especially in America, where grunge had now taken hold. As Strummer had demonstrated a decade earlier with The Clash, even the best groups tend not to recognise when they should call it a day, and after finally leaving CBS (now operating as Sony), Jones signed to his manager Gary Kurfirst's semi-independent label Radioactive, releasing the album *F-Punk* under the original name Big Audio Dynamite in 1985. Though the lead single, 'I Turned Out A Punk', has a certain simplistic nostalgic charm, the record disappeared almost without trace, and the group's next album was rejected by Radioactive out of hand. B.A.D. did not so much break up as grind to a halt.

Big Audio Dynamite left behind a full decade's worth of memorable dance parties-come-live shows, a number of classic singles under a multitude of mixes, and frequently inspired (though sometimes corny) albums. The singles compilation *Planet B.A.D.* and, though it's difficult to find, the remix collection *The Lost Treasure of Big Audio Dynamite I & II,* are excellent places to start wading through this considerable catalogue. B.A.D.'s legacy also includes a highly influential vibe that can't be fully captured in audio-visual form and of which Mick Jones deserves to be proud.

After immersing himself in The Clash remastering and reissue campaign, including the live album *From Here To Eternity* and the box set *Clash On Broadway*, Mick Jones matured into a middle-aged role as punk godfather. In that guise he came full circle, producing the first two albums by The Libertines, whose debt to 1977-era The Clash he clearly doesn't find too close for comfort.

In 2003, he formed Carbon/Silicon with life-long friend, and former Generation X/Sigue Sigue Sputnik bassist, Tony James. The group embraced the new digital technology, turning it into a major part of their manifesto, and decided that, rather than sign to a record company (or seek clearance for the many samples they had used in their recordings), they would make their music freely available as online MP3 downloads. Carbon/Silicon gave away several albums worth of material (some now available for purchase at the band's web site) before forming a fully functioning live band, and re-recording/compiling/mastering the best of these early songs as the album *The Last Post*, which was released in conventional CD format in 2007. While the music was more stripped down than that of Big Audio Dynamite – typically featuring the repetition of a simple guitar chord structure over a straight-forward programmed rhythm – the lyrics were arguably more complex, many of them allowing Jones to tell a story (or sell his resolutely positive-outlook philosophy) over the course of multiple verses, as on the stand-out tracks 'The News' and 'Oil Well.' Carbon/Silicon toured extensively on the back of *The Last Post* and followed it up in 2010 with the CD, *The Carbon Bubble*, which lacked for the same kind of enthusiasm either within the music itself or in public reaction.

It was, therefore, probably not unrelated that, early in 2011, Jones announced the reformation of Big Audio Dynamite, in its classic original five-piece line-up. The act appeared at many of the major festivals over the course of the spring and summer, the quintet all looking impressively spritely for their age. Sony/Legacy released a special edition of the debut album *This Is Big Audio Dynamite*, compiling the various 12" mixes onto a second disc, to coincide with the extensive live activity.

Topper Headon and Paul Simonon had the sort of short-lived solo careers all too familiar for non-songwriting rhythm section members. Under his own name, Headon was the first out of the blocks in June 1985, with a big band jazz cover of 'Drummin' Man'. Signed to Mercury, he then made a solo album, *Waking Up*, released in 1986, just as Big Audio Dynamite began making waves. Unsurprisingly, given Headon's musical training, it was heavy on soul, jazz and R&B, aided in no small part by stellar musicians like vocalist Jimmy Helms, guitarist and vocalist Bob Tench, and erstwhile Clash/Blockheads keyboardist Mickey Gallagher. As well as a cover of Booker T's 'Time Is Tight' (a strange choice given The Clash's own prior recording), there were several of the drummer's own compositions that addressed Headon's addictions, including 'Just Another Hit', 'Got To Keep On Going' and the single 'Pleasure and Pain', which had the makings of a hit. Reviews were positive, but Clash fans were not greatly impressed, and he lacked the commitment to build a new career from scratch. In 1987, following one heroin offence too many, Nicky Headon received a 15-month jail sentence. He has rarely played music professionally since, although rumours as to his whereabouts were finally eased when he was interviewed, gaunt and thin, for the *Westway To The World* documentary. Headon has subsequently showed up in public to accept his share of Clash awards. The loss of the drummer's talent to the evils of heroin may be a familiar rock'n'roll story, but it's a tragic one all the same: there's no doubt that The

Clash were at their recording peak while Headon was at his own pinnacle of professionalism and performance, and as 'Rock The Casbah' proved, he had the makings of a magnificent songwriter.

Paul Simonon had always been the rock solid core of The Clash. What he lacked in musical talent and intellectual curiosity he more than made up for in an onstage persona of wild abandon, and an offstage demeanor of confident cool. From the blue spiked haircut of 1977 to the Trilby-wearing rebel-without-a-cause look of the *London Calling* era and the Johnny Too Bad gangster of Strummer's home movie *Hell W10*, Simonon was seen as a man who answered to no-one but himself. So, it was no great shock that he took his time weighing up post-Clash musical options, finally surfacing with the rockabilly-tinged band Havana 3am in 1990. (The group were introduced the previous year via a shout-out on the sleeve to B.A.D.'s *Megatop Phoenix*.) He was content to hold a similar role in his new band as with The Clash: playing bass, providing backing vocals and sharing songwriting credits. Still, when Havana 3am's eponymous album was released by IRS in 1991, the label was smart enough to put Simonon's name on the front cover, which must have played its part in creating the band's healthy American following. Simonon left Havana 3am before that following could count for anything substantial, however, returning to his first love and finer talent, painting.

Simonon returned to music in 2006 to team up with Damon Albarn (Blur/Gorillaz), Simon Tong (Verve, Gorillaz) and renowned Nigerian drummer Tony Allen for a one-off album project entitled *The Good, The Bad and The Queen*. The album reached number two in the British charts and entered the *Billboard* charts just inside the Top 50. In 2008 Topper Headon joined Carbon/Silicon onstage at a show in London, and in 2010, Paul Simonon and Mick Jones appeared together on the title track of Gorillaz' third album *Plastic Beach*. They then joined the act's subsequent tour.

The weight of post-Clash expectations fell heaviest on Joe Strummer. Having embarrassed himself by sacking Mick Jones, only to lead The Clash down a musical and credible cul-de-sac with *Cut The Crap*, he spent the rest of the Eighties trying to rescue his reputation. His public reconciliation with Jones, and the accompanying songwriting and production credits on B.A.D.'s *No. 10, Upping St.* certainly helped, as did his contribution of two songs to Alex Cox's controversial 1986 punk biopic *Sid'n'Nancy.* This in turn led to Strummer appearing in Cox's next two movies, each of which seemed tailor-made for the former Clash front man. He had a starring role in *Straight To Hell*, named for the Clash song, an ill-received spaghetti western parody shot in Spain, which also starred members of The Pogues and a yet-to-be-infamous Courtney Love. He also briefly appeared in *Walker,* the story of the American mercenary who pulled off a coup in Nicaragua for his millionaire backer. In addition, Strummer provided two instrumentals to the soundtrack for *Straight To Hell* (which was re-released by Big Beat/Ace in 2004) and a fuller cinematic accompaniment to the latter (currently unavailable). Around the same time, Strummer also showed up in Robert Frank *Candy Mountain* (1987) and Jim Jarmusch's acclaimed *Mystery Train* (1989).

Having finally regained his confidence and credibility, Strummer duly embarked on his long-awaited solo album, recording with a core group of little-known musicians in Los Angeles. *Earthquake Weather*, released in 1989, lacked the passion and vitality of The Clash while seeming scared to follow through on its global music influences, and it succeeded only in presenting Joe as a mediocre Bruce Springsteen. A commercial and critical disappointment, it may have just been the wrong music at the wrong time; though the album is too long and wildly unfocused, songs such as 'Gangsterville' and 'Boogie With Your Children' would surely have had a warmer reception either a decade earlier or later.

Strummer was not the only one hit hard by the public indifference. Epic Records (whose entire staff Strummer had unexpectedly thanked on the solo album sleeve) refused to take up the option on his contract, and Strummer withdrew from the songwriting process entirely. The Nineties found him producing Shane MacGowan's group The Pogues, filling the absent alcoholic singer's place in the touring group for a while, and occasionally venturing out to DJ. The nearest he came to solo recording was with 'England's Irie', a hit single timed for the Euro 1996 football tournament, credited to Black Grape Featuring Joe Strummer And Keith Allen.

Only when the 21st Century loomed on the horizon did Strummer finally break out on his own again, and this time he did it right. He assembled a permanent band, Joe Strummer & The Mescaleros, with drummer Pablo Cook, bassist Scott Shields, guitarist Antony Genn and, on keyboards, former Black Grape member Martin Slattery. The music took a decisive step back from the Springsteen-esque solo routines of *Earthquake Weather,* expanding instead on the gypsy and global influence that had always been a part of Joe's persona. The new group had new distribution: 1999's *Rock Art and The X-Ray Style* was released on Mercury Records in the UK, and through the independent label Hellcat (owned by Tim Armstrong of Rancid, a group rooted in Seventies Clash punk) in the USA. It received a cautious reaction, critics and fans alike perhaps a little unwilling to give Strummer the benefit of the doubt yet again. But *Rock Art and The X-Ray Style* contained many splendid moments: 'Sandpaper Blues' mixed music from Africa, the Middle East and Europe in one song, 'Techno D-Day' was a rock anthem as Strummer should have written for *Earthquake Weather*, and 'The Road To Rock'n'Roll' showed him incapable of shaking his love of music mythology. (Nor had he lost his political idealism: a sleeve note dedicated the album "to all freedom fighters". The next year, accompanied by The Long Beach Dub All Stars, he covered

Jimmy Cliff's 'The Harder They Come' for a benefit album, arranged by Steve Earle, for The West Memphis 3.) The closing ballad 'Willesden To Cricklewood' – Strummer's first foray into 3/4 time since *Sandinista!*'s 'Rebel Waltz' – revealed a tenderness that could only have come with age.

Indeed, Strummer was now approaching his fiftieth birthday. Yet surrounded by the youthful Mescaleros he appeared to have found a new lease of life, and he began touring properly under his own name for the first time since The Clash. His younger compatriots found it hard to keep up with their former marathon runner leader's stamina, both on stage and off, and soon developed the phrase "You got Strummer'd" for anyone the singer dragged around town, bar-hopping till post-show closing time.

The positive mood of these good time travels was all over 2001's Global A Go-Go, with songs like 'Shaktar Donetsk', 'At The Border, Guy' and 'Bhindi Bhagee' celebrating multi-culturalism in all its musical and social glory. With Genn having gone, Scott Shields assumed guitar duties as well as bass, and Strummer's life-long friend, former busking partner, and Sandinista! guest Tymon Dogg joined on violin. Dogg's presence pushed the Romany influence to center stage, and a 17-minute closing finale 'Minstrel Boy', built around a lilting violin line, again in waltz tempo, made perfect use of the Compact Disc's extra space. As a mark of respect to another famous and influential punk, Global A Go-Go was dedicated to Joey Ramone, who passed away in 2001.

Joe Strummer turned 50 in August 2002. After the tumultuous years of The Clash and a certain amount of musical torment in the decade thereafter, his life had reached an enviable equilibrium. He was idolised by young music fans worldwide for his work a quarter of a century earlier, but he was also gaining a new following for his current output, the lower commercial expectations for which seemed to perfectly suit the freewheeling, energetic, ever-adventurous

Strummer. In live shows, The Mescaleros played a mixture of new material and Clash songs, concentrating mostly on the previous group's reggae covers, though Strummer could rarely resist throwing 'London's Burning' in for nostalgic good measure. With his show-stealing appearance in the *Westway To The World* documentary, Strummer had shown himself unabashedly proud of The Clash, maintaining a young man's zeal for personal enlightenment and social equality, and yet apparently incapable of harboring ill will. He was happily married to Lucinda – Luce on all sleeve shout-outs – and lived in a rustic home in the Somerset countryside.

In late 2002, Strummer re-convened The Mescaleros to record their third album; Simon Stafford was now playing bass, leaving Shields to concentrate on guitar, and Luke Bullen had replaced Pablo Cook on drums. Half-way through what they believed was their finest music yet, they broke for Christmas. On December 22, Strummer took his dog for a walk, came home, had a sudden heart attack and died on his kitchen floor.

The loss was felt far and wide, both within the music business and outside. The death of that other Punk Joe Public, Joey Ramone, had been sadly expected; Strummer's came as a total shock, something that made it all the more difficult to register. Several obituaries noted that the man with one of the biggest hearts in music had, perhaps, shared so much of it along the way that he left nothing in it for his old age.

There was also some understandable short-term selfishness among the many mourners: The Clash were being inducted into the Rock'n'Roll Hall of Fame in the New Year of 2003, and until Strummer's untimely death, the group had encouraged rumours that they'd be performing on stage together for the occasion. Now that would not be possible. Prior to this prestigious (if conformist) honour, The Clash had turned down several serious financial offers to re-unite and tour, which seemed all the more frustrating given that the founding trio

remained such good personal friends. On occasions when they did play together, it was usually low profile: as recently as November 2002, Mick Jones had joined Strummer on stage at a benefit for striking English firemen. It turned out to be Joe's penultimate gig.

Scott Shields and Martin Slattery were asked to finish the third Mescaleros album at the request of Joe's wife Lucinda. Inspired by the powerful ghost of Strummer's own relentless determination, they gradually worked up from the small number of barely completed songs a ten-track album, *Streetcore*. The process necessitated using several outside recordings: a demo Strummer had recorded for Johnny Cash ('Long Shadow'), a version of the Bob Marley busker's favourite 'Redemption Song' (produced by Rick Rubin), and the Danny Saber-produced dance track 'All In A Day'.

On paper, it didn't look like a complete album, but Shields and Slattery served Strummer's memory proud, and it's no posthumous nicety to say that Streetcore (released in October 2003) is Strummer's finest work since The Clash. Of the few complete Mescaleros songs, 'Coma Girl' found Strummer maintaining his life-long obsession with the mythical "gang" to a straight-forward Clash-friendly melody, 'Get Down Moses' had him revisiting the punk-reggae crossover, and the ballad 'Burning Streets' deliberately revived the theme of 'London's Burning'. Of the uncompleted songs, 'Ramshackle Day Parade' had been meticulously built underneath Joe's guide vocal, while 'Midnight Jam' took an unfinished instrumental and beamed in Strummer's voice from some BBC World Service shows he had recorded, an inspired stroke that successfully imbued the song with the singer's personality. The rambunctious 'Arms Aloft' harked back to past triumphs – "We were arms aloft in Aberdeen" – and 'All In A Day' (the Danny Sabers production) was so reminiscent of B.A.D. at their vibed-up peak that first-time listeners were convinced they were hearing Mick Jones on vocals.

Streetcore concludes with the song that had opened the recording sessions: a simple rendition of the Fats Domino favourite 'Before I Grow Too Old'. If Strummer, performing with Shields and Slattery and led by Tymon Dogg's folksy violin, hadn't intended the song's late-life lyrics to be quite so literal – "I got to hurry up before I grow too old," - he would surely have loved the way his band-mates allowed him the last word. "Okay, that's a take," we hear him happily report, directing affairs to the end. It's a magnificent epitaph.

Not long after his death, punk veteran film-maker Julien Temple, fresh from his success with the Sex Pistols documentary *The Filth and The Fury*, signed on to tell the story of Strummer's life. Don Letts' *Westway To The World* had already done an excellent job of documenting the Clash story, using extensive interviews conducted with Strummer while he was still alive, leaving Temple with a tough act to follow. The director tackled this dilemma by bringing together a vast crowd of Strummer's friends and family and placing them around a series of campfires in various global locations. (Strummer had always had a close affinity to the campfire format, especially at festivals.) This cast included the likes of Steve Jones, Damien Hirst, Bono, Steve Buscemi, Anthony Kiedis and Johnny Depp, to name but a few. The talking heads went uncredited throughout, which for all that it caused some audience confusion, allowed the focus to remain fully on the subject himself. An impressive amount of archival footage and the support of Joe's widow, Lucinda Mellor, enabled the movie to rise above the typical posthumous documentary, and to stand instead as a heart-felt tribute to a man who had such a lasting impact on so many lives.

PART V
THE CLASH
IN PRINT

As befits a group of such musical importance and lyrical incisiveness, there has been no shortage of books on The Clash. The death of Joe Strummer in December 2002 brought on a deluge of new biographies, several focused purely on the lead singer. There are also two purely photographic books on a band that rarely posed a bad photo.

D'Ambrosio, Antonino. *Let Fury Have The Hour: The Punk Rock Politics of Joe Strummer* (Nation, 2004)

Davie, Anthony. *Joe Strummer And The Mescaleros: Visions Of A Homeland* (Effective Publishing, 2004)

Gilbert, Pat. *Passion Is A Fashion: The Real Story of The Clash* (Aurum, 2004)

Gray, Marcus. *The Clash: Return of The Last Gang in Town* (Helter Skelter, 2003, originally published in 1995 as *The Last Gang In Town*, updated in 2001)

Gray, Marcus. *Route 19 Revisited: The Clash and the Making of London Calling* (Vintage, 2011)

Green, Johnny & Barker, Garry, illustrations by Ray Lowry, foreword by Joe Strummer *A Riot of Our Own: Night and Day with The Clash* (Faber & Faber, 1999).

Knowles, Chris. *Clash City Showdown* (Lightning Source, 2003; collected essays from web site of same name)

Needs, Kris. *Joe Strummer And The Legend Of The Clash* (Plexus, 2004)

Parker, Alan. *The Clash: Rat Patrol From Fort Bragg* (Abstract, 2003)

Salewicz, Chris. *Redemption Song: The Authorised Biography of Joe Strummer* (Harper Collins, 2005)

Strummer, Joe, Jones, Mick, Simonon, Paul, Headon, Tooper. *The Clash* (Atlantic Books, 2008)

Topping, Keith. *The Complete Clash* (Reynolds &Hearn, 2003)

Photo books

Gruen, Bob, with an introduction by Salewicz, Chris. *The Clash* (Vision On, 2003)

Smith, Pennie. *The Clash: Before and After* (Plexus, 1991)

BY THE SAME AUTHOR

NON-FICTION:

All Hopped Up And Ready To Go: Music From The Streets Of New York 1927-1977 (2009)*

Dear Boy: The Life Of Keith Moon (1998)

Remarks Remade: The Story of R.E.M. (1989 & 2002)

Never Stop: The Echo & The Bunnymen Story (1987)

FICTION:

Hedonism: Lust & Betrayal In New York's Clubland (2003), a crime novel set in the world of 1990s New York nightlife,

All published by Omnibus Press

Tony Fletcher's first Clash purchase was the 'Complete Control' single in 1977. He still rates it one of the best 45s of all time. He first saw The Clash play as part of the crowd that marched from Trafalgar Square to Victoria Park, Hackney, April 30, 1978, three days after he turned 14. He last saw Joe Strummer play in April 2002, in Brooklyn, New York. He can be found at www.ijamming.net.